FIBROMYALGIA COOKBOOK

MEGA BUNDLE - 7 Manuscripts in 1 - 300+ Fibromyalgia - friendly recipes for a balanced and healthy diet

TABLE OF CONTENTS

Introduction

Fibromyalgia recipes for personal enjoyment but also for family enjoyment. You will love them for sure for how easy it is to prepare them.

BREAKFAST

CHICKEN EGG ROLL

Serves: *4*

Prep Time: *10* Minutes

Cook Time: *10* Minutes

Total Time: *20* Minutes

INGREDIENTS

- **3 ½ ounces chicken breast**
- **1 dash salt**
- **½ packages stevia**
- **3 cabbage leaves**
- **1 cup shredded cabbage**
- **2 Melba toast**

DIRECTIONS

1. **Steam the cabbage leaves for 5 minutes.**
2. **Add the shredded cabbage and steam for 5 minutes.**
3. **Place the cabbage in a bowl along with the chicken and the spices.**
4. **Wrap the mixture in cabbage leaves and serve topped with Melba toast.**

MORNING CUPS

Serves: *12*

Prep Time: *10* Minutes

Cook Time: *30* Minutes

Total Time: *40* Minutes

INGREDIENTS

- 1 cup cheese
- 8 eggs
- ¼ cup water
- 1 handful spinach
- 10 slices bacon
- ½ tbs Dijon mustard
- 1 tsp hot sauce
- Salt
- Pepper

DIRECTIONS

1. Preheat the oven to 350F.
2. Divide the spinach, cheese, and bacon into 12 greased cups of a cupcake tin.
3. Whisk together the water, eggs, mustard, hot sauce, salt, and pepper in a bowl.
4. Fill the cups with the egg mixture within 1/4 -inch from top.

5. **Stir each cup, then bake for 30 minutes.**
6. **Serve hot.**

EGG BAKE

Serves: ***4***

Prep Time: ***10*** Minutes

Cook Time: ***40*** Minutes

Total Time: ***50*** Minutes

INGREDIENTS

- **4 eggs**
- **¾ cup cheese**
- **½ rice avocado**
- **Sour cream**
- **½ onion**
- **6 bacon strips**
- **1 can diced tomatoes**
- **½ tsp cayenne pepper**
- **4 egg whites**
- **Hot sauce**
- **½ red bell pepper**
- **½ green bell pepper**

DIRECTIONS

1. **Whisk the eggs with the egg whites and cayenne pepper in a bowl.**
2. **Saute the onions, peppers and bacon until cooked.**

3. **Mix the tomatoes, cheese, egg and pepper mixture together in a baking dish.**
4. **Bake for 40 minutes.**
5. **Serve topped with avocado, sour cream and hot sauce.**

BREAKFAST CASSEROLE

Serves: ***4***

Prep Time: ***10*** Minutes

Cook Time: ***40*** Minutes

Total Time: ***50*** Minutes

INGREDIENTS

- **2 poblano chile peppers**
- **12 ounces chicken sausage**
- **½ tsp garlic powder**
- **½ tsp onion powder**
- **½ tsp salt**
- **2 garlic cloves**
- **12 egg whites**
- **4 eggs**
- **1 cup milk**
- **2 tbs cilantro**
- **½ tsp black pepper**
- **¼ cup green onion**
- **1 tsp olive oil**
- **½ onion**
- **4 oz. cheddar cheese**
- **Oil**
- **Sour cream**

- 1 tsp hot sauce
- ½ tsp chili powder
- ½ red bell pepper

DIRECTIONS

1. Preheat the oven to 350F.
2. Roast the poblanos.
3. Place the peppers aside until cool enough to handle.
4. Peel the skin off and remove the seeds and stems.
5. Place the peppers in a greased baking dish.
6. Cook the chicken sausage until brown.
7. Remove from heat and spoon over the peppers.
8. Saute the onion and bell peppers in the oil.
9. Add the garlic and stir for a minute.
10. Spoon the mixture over the poblanos.
11. Top with the green onions and cilantro.
12. Whisk the eggs, egg whites, chili powder, onion powder, hot sauce, garlic powder, milk, salt, and pepper in a bowl.
13. Pour into baking dish, coating all of the ingredients.
14. Add cheese on top.
15. Bake for 30 minutes, remove and serve

SCOTCH EGGS

Serves: *6*

Prep Time: *10* Minutes

Cook Time: *40* Minutes

Total Time: *50* Minutes

INGREDIENTS

- 1 lb breakfast sausage
- 6 hard-boiled eggs
- ¼ cup flour
- 1 egg
- 1 ½ cups panko bread crumbs
- 4 tbs oil

DIRECTIONS

1. Preheat the oven to 350F.
2. Divide the sausage into 6 portions.
3. Wrap the eggs with the sausage.
4. Roll them into flour, egg wash, and panko crumbs in this order.
5. Preheat the oil in a pan.
6. Cook the balls until brown on all sides.
7. Place on a tray.
8. Bake for 25 minutes, remove and serve

SUNNY-SIDE UP EGG

Serves: ***4***

Prep Time: ***10*** Minutes

Cook Time: ***10*** Minutes

Total Time: ***20*** Minutes

INGREDIENTS

- **1 egg**
- **6 tbs egg whites**
- **¼ spinach**
- **3 tbs green onion**
- **Salt**
- **Pepper**

DIRECTIONS

1. **Preheat the burner.**
2. **Grease a skillet with cooking spray.**
3. **Crack the egg into the skillet and add 6 tbs egg whites.**

EGG WHITE TOSTADA

Serves: *1*

Prep Time: *5* Minutes

Cook Time: *5* Minutes

Total Time: *10* Minutes

INGREDIENTS

- 2 toast
- ½ tsp cilantro
- Pepper
- 1 egg white
- 1 tsp salsa
- 2 tbs water
- Salt

DIRECTIONS

1. Cook the egg white in a pan, then season with salt and pepper and add 1 tbs water.
2. Cook for ½ minute covered.
3. Divide in 2 and place each half on the toast.
4. Top with salsa and cilantro.

BREAKFAST SCRAMBLE

Serves: *1*

Prep Time: *5* Minutes

Cook Time: *5* Minutes

Total Time: ***10*** Minutes

INGREDIENTS

- **5 tbs salsa**
- **1 egg**
- **5 tbs egg substitute**
- **Salt**
- **Pepper**

DIRECTIONS

1. **Scramble the eggs.**
2. **Add the egg substitute and cook.**
3. **Season with salt and pepper.**
4. **Serve topped with salsa.**

BREAKFAST PIZZA

Serves: 2
Prep Time: *5* Minutes

Cook Time: *10* Minutes

Total Time: *15* Minutes

INGREDIENTS

- 1 egg
- 2 egg whites
- Cheese
- Salt
- Red pepper
- Tomatoes
- Milk
- Mushrooms
- Pepper
- Green pepper

DIRECTIONS

1. **Whisk the eggs, egg whites, and milk together.**
2. **Cook in a skillet for 3 minutes.**
3. **When almost set, top with the vegetables and add cheese on top.**
4. **Serve immediately.**

FRENCH TOAST

Serves: *4*

Prep Time: *10* Minutes

Cook Time: *10* Minutes

Total Time: *20* Minutes

INGREDIENTS

- **Bread slices**
- **Egg substitute**
- **1 tsp cinnamon**
- **Stevia**
- **1 tsp vanilla**
- **Butter**

DIRECTIONS

1. **Mix the egg substitute, vanilla, and cinnamon in a bowl.**
2. **Melt the butter in a skillet.**
3. **Coat the bread slices with the egg mixture.**
4. **Cook until golden.**
5. **Serve immediately.**

SPANICH OMELET

Serves: 2

Prep Time: *10* Minutes

Cook Time: *10* Minutes

Total Time: *20* Minutes

INGREDIENTS

- **6 eggs**
- **1 ½ cups bell peppers**
- **1 onion**
- **Salt**
- **Pepper**
- **Thyme**
- **1 can potatoes**

DIRECTIONS

1. **Whisk the eggs together in a bowl.**
2. **Season and add the vegetables.**
3. **Cook until fluffy.**
4. **Serve hot.**

APPLE CRUMB CAKE

Serves: ***4***

Prep Time: ***10*** Minutes

Cook Time: ***30*** Minutes

Total Time: ***40*** Minutes

INGREDIENTS

Cake

- **1 egg**
- **1 cup flour**
- **1 tsp baking soda**
- **½ cup yogurt**
- **½ cup apple sauce**
- **1 cup brown sugar**
- **1 tsp vanilla**
- **1 ½ cups apple cored**

Topping

- **3 tbs brown sugar**
- **3 tbs flour**
- **1 tbs butter**

DIRECTIONS

1. **Mix all of the cake ingredients in a bowl.**
2. **Place on a baking sheet.**
3. **Mix the topping ingredients, then add over the cake.**

4. **Bake for 30 minutes.**
5. **Allow to cool, then serve.**

BREAKFAST QUINOA

Serves: 2

Prep Time: *10* Minutes

Cook Time: *20* Minutes

Total Time: *30* Minutes

INGREDIENTS

- **2 tbs water**
- **1 tbs brown sugar**
- **¼ cup coconut flakes**
- **1 cup bananas**
- **½ cup quinoa**
- **¾ cup coconut milk**
- **1 cup strawberries**

DIRECTIONS

1. **Cook the quinoa.**
2. **When half done, add the coconut milk and sugar and mix well.**
3. **Cook until done.**
4. **Toast the coconut flakes.**
5. **Serve topped with fruits and flakes.**

BREAKFAST TACOS

Serves: 2

Prep Time: *10* Minutes

Cook Time: *10* Minutes

Total Time: *20* Minutes

INGREDIENTS

- 2 tortillas
- 2 cups spinach leaves
- 4 eggs
- Oil
- 1 tsp cumin
- Cilantro
- Hot sauce
- 1 tsp turmeric
- ½ cup beans
- Salt
- Pepper

DIRECTIONS

1. **Cook the beans with the hot sauce and spices.**
2. **Garnish with cilantro.**
3. **Fry the spinach leaves.**

4. **Scramble the eggs.**
5. **Add the beans, eggs and spinach leaves on the tortillas.**
6. **Serve topped with avocado slices and garnished with cilantro.**

BLUEBERRY OATS

Serves: **2**

Prep Time: *5* Minutes

Cook Time: ***10*** Minutes

Total Time: ***15*** Minutes

INGREDIENTS

- **2 cups blueberries**
- **1 tsp lemon rind**
- **1 tbs lemon juice**
- **1 cup oats**
- **¼ cup brown sugar**
- **½ tsp cinnamon powder**
- **4 cups water**
- **Salt**

DIRECTIONS

1. **Prepare the compote.**
2. **Prepare the oats.**
3. **Serve the oats with the compote.**

MUSHROOM OMELETTE

Serves: *1*

Prep Time: *5* Minutes

Cook Time: *10* Minutes

Total Time: *15* Minutes

INGREDIENTS

- 2 eggs
- ¼ tsp salt
- ¼ tsp black pepper
- 1 tablespoon olive oil
- ¼ cup cheese
- ¼ tsp basil
- 1 cup mushrooms

DIRECTIONS

1. **In a bowl combine all ingredients together and mix well**
2. **In a skillet heat olive oil and pour the egg mixture**
3. **Cook for 1-2 minutes per side**
4. **When ready remove omelette from the skillet and serve**

OVERNIGHT OATMEAL

Serves: *8*

Prep Time: *10* Minutes

Cook Time: *6* Hours

Total Time: *40* Minutes

INGREDIENTS

- 7 cups water
- 1/3 cup apricots
- 2 cups of oats
- 2/3 cup cranberries

DIRECTIONS

1. **Mix the ingredients together in a slow cooker**
2. **Cook on low for at least 6 hours**

MORNING FRITTATA

Serves: 2

Prep Time: *10* Minutes

Cook Time: *15* Minutes

Total Time: *25* Minutes

INGREDIENTS

- 1/3 chicken broth
- 1 green onion
- 1 garlic clove
- Salt
- Pepper
- Herbs
- 2 tomatoes
- 1 ½ cups spinach
- 4 eggs
- 5 slices bacon

DIRECTIONS

1. Preheat oven to 350 F
2. Fry the bacon
3. Mix the eggs, broth and seasonings together well
4. Place the spinach at the bottom of a skillet and pour the batter over
5. Add the remaining ingredients, bake for 15 minutes

EGGS AND VEGETABLES

Serves: ***4***

Prep Time: ***10*** Minutes

Cook Time: ***10*** Minutes

Total Time: ***20*** Minutes

INGREDIENTS

- **2-3 tbs oil**
- **1 garlic clove**
- **Pepper**
- **1 cup green beans**
- **2 lb potatoes**
- **Salt**
- **4 eggs**

DIRECTIONS

1. **Peel and dice the potatoes then boil until starting to soften**
2. **Dice the green beans and cook for almost 5 minutes then drain**
3. **Cook the potatoes in hot oil until crispy then add the green beans and the garlic**
4. **Crack the eggs over and cook covered for at least 5 minutes**
5. **Season and serve**

TUNA SANDWICH

Serves: ***4***

Prep Time: *5* Minutes

Cook Time: *5* Minutes

Total Time: ***10*** Minutes

INGREDIENTS

- **Mayonnaise**
- **Salt**
- **Pepper**
- **Bread**
- **1 tuna tin**
- **Celery**

DIRECTIONS

1. **Mix the tuna, mayonnaise and celery together then season**
2. **Toast the bread**
3. **Spread the tuna mixture over the bread and serve**

ZUCCHINI BREAD

Serves: ***4***

Prep Time: ***10*** Minutes

Cook Time: ***40*** Minutes

Total Time: ***50*** Minutes

INGREDIENTS

- **4 tbs honey**
- **5 tbs oil**
- **1 ½ tsp baking soda**
- **3 eggs**
- **½ cup walnuts**
- **2 ½ cups flour**
- **4 Medjool dates**
- **1 banana**
- **2 tsp mixed spice**
- **1 ½ cup zucchini**

DIRECTIONS

1. **Preheat the oven to 350 F**
2. **Chop the dates and the walnuts**
3. **Mix the flour, spice and baking soda together**
4. **Mix the eggs and banana in a food processor then add remaining ingredients and mix**

5. **Pour the batter into a pan and cook for at least 40 minutes**
6. **Allow to cool then serve**

MORNING PORRIDGE

Serves: *1*
Prep Time: *5* Minutes

Cook Time: *5* Minutes

Total Time: *10* Minutes

INGREDIENTS

- Porridge
- Honey
- Blueberries
- Almonds
- 1 banana
- Chia seeds

DIRECTIONS

1. **Mix everything together**
2. **Serve drizzled with honey**

PANCAKES

BANANA PANCAKES

Serves: *4*

Prep Time: *10* Minutes

Cook Time: *20* Minutes

Total Time: *30* Minutes

INGREDIENTS

- **1 cup whole wheat flour**
- **¼ tsp baking soda**
- **¼ tsp baking powder**
- **1 cup mashed banana**
- **2 eggs**
- **1 cup milk**

DIRECTIONS

1. **In a bowl combine all ingredients together and mix well**
2. **In a skillet heat olive oil**
3. **Pour ¼ of the batter and cook each pancake for 1-2 minutes per side**
4. **When ready remove from heat and serve**

FLUFFY GREEK YOGURT PANCAKES

Serves: ***4***

Prep Time: ***10*** Minutes

Cook Time: ***10*** Minutes

Total Time: ***20*** Minutes

INGREDIENTS

- **1 egg**
- **2 cups berries**
- **2 tsp baking soda**
- **2 cups Greek yogurt**
- **½ tsp salt**
- **1 tsp vanilla**
- **2 ½ tbs maple syrup**
- **1 ½ cup flour**

DIRECTIONS

1. **Mix well the ingredients in a bowl.**
2. **Cook the pancakes in a skillet for 3 minutes on each side.**
3. **Serve topped with maple syrup.**

PUMPKIN PANCAKES

Serves: *7*

Prep Time: *10* Minutes

Cook Time: *10* Minutes

Total Time: *20* Minutes

INGREDIENTS

- **1 cup flour**
- **1/3 cup flax seed meal**
- **1/3 cup milk**
- **1 ½ tbs oil**
- **1 tsp lemon juice**
- **2 tsp cinnamon**
- **2 eggs**
- **½ ts ginger**
- **2 tbs honey**
- **½ tsp nutmeg**
- **2/3 cup pureed pumpkin**
- **2/7 tsp cloves**
- **1/3 tsp baking soda**

DIRECTIONS

1. **Mix the dry ingredients together in a bowl**
2. **Mix the wet ingredients together in another bowl**

3. **Mix the ingredients by adding the dry ingredients to the wet ones to form a batter**
4. **Heat the oil in a skillet and pour the batter using a small ladle**
5. **Fry until gold**

PANCAKES

Serves: *8*

Prep Time: *10* Minutes

Cook Time: *15* Minutes

Total Time: *25* Minutes

INGREDIENTS

- **1 egg**
- **½ tsp vanilla**
- **½ tsp baking powder**
- **Salt**
- **½ tsp flour**
- **Cinnamon**
- **Stevia**
- **½ cup water**

DIRECTIONS

1. **Mix all of the ingredients and form a batter.**
2. **Fry in coconut oil.**
3. **Serve with your favorite toppings.**

COOKIES

BREAKFAST COOKIES

Serves: *8-12*

Prep Time: *5* Minutes

Cook Time: *15* Minutes

Total Time: *20* Minutes

INGREDIENTS

- **1 cup rolled oats**
- **¼ cup applesauce**
- **½ tsp vanilla extract**
- **3 tablespoons chocolate chips**
- **2 tablespoons dried fruits**
- **1 tsp cinnamon**

DIRECTIONS

1. **Preheat the oven to 325 F**
2. **In a bowl combine all ingredients together and mix well**
3. **Scoop cookies using an ice cream scoop**
4. **Place cookies onto a prepared baking sheet**
5. **Place in the oven for 12-15 minutes or until the cookies are done**
6. **When ready remove from the oven and serve**

BREAKFAST BISCUITS

Serves: *6*

Prep Time: *5* Minutes

Cook Time: *15* Minutes

Total Time: *20* Minutes

INGREDIENTS

- 6 tbs milk
- 3 tbs water
- 3 tbs mayonnaise
- 1 cup flour

DIRECTIONS

1. **Mix the ingredients except for the mayo in a bowl.**
2. **Add in the mayonnaise and mix.**
3. **Stir in the water and milk.**
4. **Form balls and place on a baking sheet.**
5. **Bake for 15 minutes.**
6. **Serve immediately.**

SMOOTHIES

BERRY SMOOTHIE

Serves: ***4***

Prep Time: *5* Minutes

Cook Time: *5* Minutes

Total Time: ***10*** Minutes

INGREDIENTS

- **½ cup strawberries**
- **½ cup blueberries**
- **½ cup cranberries**
- **½ cup raspberries**
- **1 cup milk**
- **1 banana**
- **3 cubes ice**

DIRECTIONS

1. **In a blender place all ingredients and blend until smooth**
2. **Pour smoothie in a glass and serve**

PEACHY SMOOTHIE

Serves:	2	
Prep Time:	5	Minutes
Cook Time:	5	Minutes
Total Time:	*10*	Minutes

INGREDIENTS

- **1 peach**
- **½ cup tofu**
- **1 tablespoon sugar**
- **1 cup milk**
- **1 cup raspberries**

DIRECTIONS

1. **In a blender place all ingredients and blend until smooth**
2. **Pour smoothie in a glass and serve**

APPLE SMOOTHIE

Serves: *1*

Prep Time: *5* Minutes

Cook Time: *5* Minutes

Total Time: *10* Minutes

INGREDIENTS

- ½ cup banana
- ½ cup yogurt
- ½ cup applesauce
- ½ cup milk

DIRECTIONS

1. **In a blender place all ingredients and blend until smooth**
2. **Pour smoothie in a glass and serve**

CHERRY-LICIOUS SMOOTHIE

Serves: 2

Prep Time: 5 Minutes

Cook Time: 5 Minutes

Total Time: *10* Minutes

INGREDIENTS

- **½ cup cherries**
- **1 apple**
- **½ cup yogurt**
- **1 tablespoon agave syrup**
- **2 ice cubes**

DIRECTIONS

1. **Peel the cherries and apple and cut them into small cubes**
2. **In a blender place all ingredients and blend until smooth**
3. **Pour smoothie in a glass and serve**

CARROT SMOOTHIE

Serves: 2

Prep Time: 5 Minutes

Cook Time: 5 Minutes

Total Time: *10* Minutes

INGREDIENTS

- 2 apples
- 5 baby carrots
- 1 orange
- 1 cup spinach

DIRECTIONS

1. **In a blender place all ingredients and blend until smooth**
2. **Pour smoothie in a glass and serve**

PINEAPPLE SMOOTHIE

Serves:	2	
Prep Time:	5	Minutes
Cook Time:	5	Minutes
Total Time:	*10*	Minutes

INGREDIENTS

- **1 cup pineapple**
- **2 cups blueberries**
- **1 tablespoon sugar**
- **½ cup water**

DIRECTIONS

1. **In a blender place all ingredients and blend until smooth**
2. **Pour smoothie in a glass and serve**

PEAR SMOOTHIE

Serves: 2

Prep Time: 5 Minutes

Cook Time: 5 Minutes

Total Time: *10* Minutes

INGREDIENTS

- 1 banana
- 1 pear
- 1 apple
- 1 cup yogurt
- 2 tablespoons seeds

DIRECTIONS

1. In a blender place all ingredients and blend until smooth
2. Pour smoothie in a glass and serve

MANGO SMOOTHIE

Serves: *1*

Prep Time: *5* Minutes

Cook Time: *5* Minutes

Total Time: *10* Minutes

INGREDIENTS

- **1 cup mango**
- **1 cup pineapple**
- **2 cups spinach**
- **½ cup water**

DIRECTIONS

1. **In a blender place all ingredients and blend until smooth**
2. **Pour smoothie in a glass and serve**

MUFFINS

SIMPLE MUFFINS

Serves: *8-12*

Prep Time: *10* Minutes

Cook Time: *20* Minutes

Total Time: *30* Minutes

INGREDIENTS

- 2 eggs
- 1 tablespoon olive oil
- 1 cup milk
- 2 cups whole wheat flour
- 1 tsp baking soda
- ¼ tsp baking soda
- 1 cup pumpkin puree
- 1 tsp cinnamon
- ¼ cup molasses

DIRECTIONS

1. **In a bowl combine all dry ingredients**
2. **In another bowl combine all dry ingredients**
3. **Combine wet and dry ingredients together**
4. **Pour mixture into 8-12 prepared muffin cups, fill 2/3 of the cups**

5. Bake for 18-20 minutes at 375 F
6. When ready remove from the oven and serve

CRANBERRY MUFFINS

Serves: *12*

Prep Time: *5* Minutes

Cook Time: *25* Minutes

Total Time: *30* Minutes

INGREDIENTS

- 1 ½ cups flour
- 1 tsp baking soda
- 1/8 tsp cloves
- 1 cup brown sugar
- 1 cup pumpkin puree
- 1 tsp ginger
- 1/3 cup milk
- 1 egg
- 2 tbs oil
- ½ cup cranberries
- ½ tsp cinnamon
- 1/3 tsp baking powder
- Salt

DIRECTIONS

1. Pulse all of the ingredients in a food processor.

2. **Pour the batter into 12 muffin cups.**
3. **Bake for 25 minutes.**
4. **Serve warm.**

BANANA MUFFINS

Serves: *4*

Prep Time: *10* Minutes

Cook Time: *30* Minutes

Total Time: *40* Minutes

INGREDIENTS

- 2 cups flour
- 2 bananas
- 1 egg
- 1 tsp baking soda
- 2 tsp cinnamon
- 1 tsp baking powder
- 1/3 cup oats
- 2 tbs honey
- 1 cup milk

DIRECTIONS

1. **Preheat the oven to 350 F**
2. **Mix well the eggs, honey, milk, and banana in a bowl**
3. **Separately, mix the flour, baking soda, baking powder, oats and cinnamon.**
4. **Combine the eggs mixture and the flour mixture together gently**
5. **Pour into the muffin tray and bake until golden**

CARROT MUFFINS

Serves: *12*

Prep Time: *15* Minutes

Cook Time: *30* Minutes

Total Time: *45* Minutes

INGREDIENTS

- **1/3 cup flour**
- **1 ½ tsp nutmeg**
- **½ tp vinegar**
- **4 carrots**
- **3 tbs butter**
- **½ tsp molasses**
- **1 cup butter**
- **1 egg**
- **10 dates**
- **¼ tsp salt**
- **1 tsp baking soda**
- **1 banana**

DIRECTIONS

1. **Preheat the oven to 350 F**
2. **Whisk the egg in a bowl then add 3 tb of melted butter and mix well**

3. **Chop the dates well to form a paste**
4. **Mix the date paste, mashed banana, nutmeg, molasses, and melted butter**
5. **Add the mixture over the egg**
6. **Add the flour, mix then add the baking soda and vinegar**
7. **Pour the batter into a lined muffin pan**
8. **Allow to cool then serve**

EGG MUFFINS

Serves: *12*
Prep Time: *10* Minutes

Cook Time: *30* Minutes

Total Time: *40* Minutes

INGREDIENTS

- **Vegetables**
- **Meat**
- **1 ½ tsp seasoning**
- **12 eggs**
- **12 muffin tin liners**
- **1 cup cheese**

DIRECTIONS

1. **Place the diced meat and vegetables and cheese in the bottom of the muffin cups.**
2. **Beat the eggs and season in a bowl.**
3. **Pour the eggs into the cups and bake for 30 minutes.**
4. **Serve hot.**

SECOND COOKBOOK

BREAKFAST RECIPES

MUSHROOM OMELETTE

Serves: *1*

Prep Time: *5* Minutes

Cook Time: *5* Minutes

Total Time: *10* Minutes

INGREDIENTS

- **2 eggs**
- **Bacon**
- **2 tsp coconut oil**
- **Nutmeg**
- **1 red onion**
- **Salt**
- **Pepper**

DIRECTIONS

1. **Sauté the onion in the coconut oil for a few minutes.**
2. **Slice the mushrooms and add them to the pan, with salt and nutmeg.**
3. **Cook for another few minutes.**
4. **Remove the mushrooms from the pan.**
5. **Cook the beaten eggs for 3 minutes.**

6. **Serve the omelette topped with the mushroom mixture and bacon.**

AVOCADO TOAST

Serves: *1*

Prep Time: *5* Minutes

Cook Time: *10* Minutes

Total Time: *15* Minutes

INGREDIENTS

- **1 clove garlic**
- **½ avocado**
- **1 egg**
- **Salt**
- **1 slice toast**
- **Pepper**
- **Red pepper flakes**

DIRECTIONS

1. **Grate ½ clove of garlic into a pan, add the egg on top and cook the desired degree of doneness.**
2. **Toast the bread.**
3. **Smash the avocado with a fork.**
4. **Spread the avocado over the toast.**
5. **Top with the fried egg and garlic, season, and serve.**

TOMATO SHAKSHUKA

Serves: *4*

Prep Time: *10* Minutes

Cook Time: *50* Minutes

Total Time: *60* Minutes

INGREDIENTS

- **1 pinch cayenne**
- **Salt**
- **1 red bell pepper**
- **4 eggs**
- **¼ cup olive oil**
- **1 tbs cumin seeds**
- **1 yellow onion**
- **2 thyme sprigs**
- **1 tbs parsley**
- **1 ½ lb cherry tomatoes**

DIRECTIONS

1. **Preheat the oven to 350F.**
2. **Cut the tomatoes and place them on a cookie sheet, then season with salt.**
3. **Bake until fully roasted.**
4. **Roast the cumin seeds for 1 minute.**

5. **Add the olive oil and onion and saute until soft.**
6. **Add the strips chopped pepper, chopped herbs, and tomatoes.**
7. **Add the salt and cayenne pepper.**
8. **Pour the eggs into the pan and cook on low until the egg white i set.**
9. **Serve immediately.**

PORTOBELLO MUSHROOM CAPS

Serves: *1*

Prep Time: *5* Minutes

Cook Time: *5* Minutes

Total Time: *10* Minutes

INGREDIENTS

- 50g ham
- Salt
- Pepper
- ¼ cup watercress
- 1 Portobello mushroom
- 1 poached egg
- ½ avocado

DIRECTIONS

1. Cook the mushrooms in coconut oil for 1 minute per side.
2. Season with salt and set aside.
3. Poach the eggs.
4. Pot each Portobello cap with the sliced avocado, a handful of watercress leaves, and ham.
5. Place the egg over, sprinkle with salt and pepper and serve.

EGG IN AVOCADO

Serves: 2

Prep Time: *5* Minutes

Cook Time: *10* Minutes

Total Time: *15* Minutes

INGREDIENTS

- **1 avocado**
- **2 eggs**
- **Cheese**
- **Salt**
- **Pepper**

DIRECTIONS

1. **Preheat the oven to 425F.**
2. **Slice the avocado in half and remove the pit.**
3. **Crave out a little space in the center and crack the egg there.**
4. **Top with cheese.**
5. **Cook until the cheese is melted and the egg is done.**
6. **Serve immediately.**

OMELETTE BITES

Serves: *12*

Prep Time: *5* Minutes

Cook Time: *35* Minutes

Total Time: ***40*** Minutes

INGREDIENTS

- 4 eggs
- 1 green pepper
- 2 cups diced cooked chicken
- 2 cups spinach
- 1 avocado
- 12 egg whites
- Pepper
- 12 slices bacon
- 1 red pepper

DIRECTIONS

1. Preheat the oven to 350F.
2. Cook the bacon for 5 minutes, making sure it's not crispy.
3. Grease a muffin tin and place one piece of bacon in each tin, wrapping it around the outer edges.
4. Whisk together in a bowl the eggs, egg whites, salt, pepper, peppers, chicken, and spinach.

5. **Mix well then pour into each muffin tin.**
6. **Bake for 30 minutes, serve topped with avocado.**

MACADAMIA WAFFLES

Serves: *6*

Prep Time: *10* Minutes

Cook Time: *3* Minutes

Total Time: *40* Minutes

INGREDIENTS

- 4 tbs coconut flour
- 1 cup macadamia nuts
- ½ cup coconut milk
- 1 tsp baking powder
- 3 eggs
- 1 tsp vanilla
- 3 tbs maple syrup
- 3 tbs coconut oil

DIRECTIONS

1. Preheat the waffle iron.
2. Blend all of the ingredients for 30 seconds on low.
3. Blend on high for another 30 seconds, until completely smooth.
4. Pour the batter into the waffle iron.
5. Cook on low for 50 seconds.
6. Serve topped with your desired syrups.

BACON & AVOCADO SANDWICHES

Serves: 2

Prep Time: 5 Minutes

Cook Time: 5 Minutes

Total Time: ***10*** Minutes

INGREDIENTS

- **Salt**
- **1 avocado**
- **4 strips bacon**
- **1 lime**

DIRECTIONS

1. **Cook the bacon.**
2. **Mash the avocado with lime juice and salt.**
3. **Place the avocado mixture between the bacon slices.**
4. **Serve immediately.**

ZUCCHINI FRITTATA

Serves: ***4***

Prep Time: ***10*** Minutes

Cook Time: ***25*** Minutes

Total Time: ***35*** Minutes

INGREDIENTS

- **1 sweet potato**
- **2 zucchinis**
- **8 eggs**
- **1 red bell pepper**
- **2 tbs coconut oil**
- **2 tbs parsley**
- **Salt**
- **Pepper**

DIRECTIONS

1. **Cook the potato slices in the oil for 10 minutes.**
2. **Add the zucchini and bell peppers and cook for another 5 minutes.**
3. **Whisk the eggs in a bowl.**
4. **Season with salt and pepper and add it to the veggies.**
5. **Cook on low for 10 minutes.**
6. **Serve topped with fresh parsley.**

SWEET POTATO BREAKFAST CAKE

Serves: **4**

Prep Time: *30* Minutes

Cook Time: *15* Minutes

Total Time: *35* Minutes

INGREDIENTS

- **2 tbs oil**
- **2 tbs parsley**
- **1 red onion**
- **3 egg whites**
- **2 sweet potatoes**
- **½ cup dried cranberries**
- **6 eggs**
- **Salt**
- **Pepper**

DIRECTIONS

1. **Preheat the oven to 425F.**
2. **Poke holes all around the potatoes using a fork.**
3. **Add the cranberries, parsley, onion, salt, and pepper.**
4. **Add 2 whisked egg whites.**
5. **Make patties from the mixture.**
6. **Cook in oil for 4 minutes on each side.**

7. Place the cooked patties onto a greased baking dish.
8. Push down in the middle of each patty, creating space for the eggs.
9. Crack the eggs on top, into the created space.
10. Bake for 15 minutes.
11. Caramelize the onion in a skillet.
12. Serve topped with the caramelized onions.

MINI EGG OMELETS

Serves: *4*

Prep Time: *10* Minutes

Cook Time: *20* Minutes

Total Time: *30* Minutes

INGREDIENTS

- **¼ cup shredded cheddar**
- **4 eggs**
- **¼ cup cheese**
- **1 ½ tsp olive oil**
- **4 cups broccoli florets**
- **Salt**
- **Pepper**
- **1 cup egg whites**

DIRECTIONS

1. **Preheat the oven to 350F.**
2. **Steam the broccoli for 5 minutes.**
3. **Once cooked, crumble into smaller pieces and add olive oil, sal and pepper.**
4. **Grease a muffin tin and pour the mixture into each tin.**
5. **Beat the egg whites, eggs, cheese, salt and pepper in a bowl.**
6. **Pour over the broccoli, top with cheese and cook for 20 minutes**

BREAKFAST MEATCAKES

Serves: ***14***

Prep Time: ***10*** Minutes

Cook Time: ***40*** Minutes

Total Time: ***50*** Minutes

INGREDIENTS

- **1 lb pork sausage**
- **6 ounces blackberries**
- **1 tsp cinnamon**
- **1 ½ tsp salt**
- **1 tsp black pepper**
- **1 tsp rosemary**
- **1 tsp thyme**
- **1 orange zest**
- **1 ln chicken breast**
- **12 strips bacon**
- **1 apple**
- **1 tsp garlic powder**

DIRECTIONS

1. **Preheat the oven to 375F.**
2. **Dice the apple.**
3. **Line the cupcake pans with bacon.**

4. **Mix together, smashing with hands, sausage, spices, chicken, apple, zest, and blackberries.**
5. **Fill the pan with the mixture.**
6. **Bake for 35 minutes.**
7. **Serve topped with zest or blackberries.**

CANTALOUPE PANCAKES

Serves: ***4***

Prep Time: ***10*** Minutes

Cook Time: ***20*** Minutes

Total Time: ***30*** Minutes

INGREDIENTS

- **1 cup whole wheat flour**
- **¼ tsp baking soda**
- **¼ tsp baking powder**
- **2 eggs**
- **1 cup milk**
- **1 cup cantaloupe**

DIRECTIONS

1. **In a bowl combine all ingredients together and mix well**
2. **In a skillet heat olive oil**
3. **Pour ¼ of the batter and cook each pancake for 1-2 minutes per side**
4. **When ready remove from heat and serve**

COCONUT PANCAKES

Serves: *4*

Prep Time: *10* Minutes

Cook Time: *20* Minutes

Total Time: *30* Minutes

INGREDIENTS

- **1 cup whole wheat flour**
- **¼ tsp baking soda**
- **¼ tsp baking powder**
- **1 cup coconut flalkes**
- **2 eggs**
- **1 cup milk**

DIRECTIONS

1. **In a bowl combine all ingredients together and mix well**
2. **In a skillet heat olive oil**
3. **Pour ¼ of the batter and cook each pancake for 1-2 minutes per side**
4. **When ready remove from heat and serve**

CHERRIES PANCAKES

Serves: *4*

Prep Time: *10* Minutes

Cook Time: *30* Minutes

Total Time: *40* Minutes

INGREDIENTS

- **1 cup whole wheat flour**
- **¼ tsp baking soda**
- **¼ tsp baking powder**
- **2 eggs**
- **1 cup milk**
- **1 cup cherries**

DIRECTIONS

1. **In a bowl combine all ingredients together and mix well**
2. **In a skillet heat olive oil**
3. **Pour ¼ of the batter and cook each pancake for 1-2 minutes per side**
4. **When ready remove from heat and serve**

MANGO MUFFINS

Serves: *8-12*

Prep Time: *10* Minutes

Cook Time: *20* Minutes

Total Time: *30* Minutes

INGREDIENTS

- 2 eggs
- 1 tablespoon olive oil
- 1 cup milk
- 2 cups whole wheat flour
- 1 tsp baking soda
- ¼ tsp baking soda
- 1 tsp ginger
- 1 tsp cinnamon
- 1 cup mango

DIRECTIONS

1. In a bowl combine all wet ingredients
2. In another bowl combine all dry ingredients
3. Combine wet and dry ingredients together
4. Pour mixture into 8-12 prepared muffin cups, fill 2/3 of the cups
5. Bake for 18-20 minutes at 375 F, when ready remove and serve

NECTARINE MUFFINS

Serves: *8-12*

Prep Time: *10* Minutes

Cook Time: *20* Minutes

Total Time: *30* Minutes

INGREDIENTS

- 2 eggs
- 1 tablespoon olive oil
- 1 cup milk
- 2 cups whole wheat flour
- 1 tsp baking soda
- ¼ tsp baking soda
- 1 tsp cinnamon
- 1 cup nectarine

DIRECTIONS

1. In a bowl combine all wet ingredients
2. In another bowl combine all dry ingredients
3. Combine wet and dry ingredients together
4. Pour mixture into 8-12 prepared muffin cups, fill 2/3 of the cups
5. Bake for 18-20 minutes at 375 F
6. When ready remove from the oven and serve

PAPAYA MUFFINS

Serves: *8-12*

Prep Time: *10* Minutes

Cook Time: *20* Minutes

Total Time: *30* Minutes

INGREDIENTS

- 2 eggs
- 1 tablespoon olive oil
- 1 cup milk
- 2 cups whole wheat flour
- 1 tsp baking soda
- ¼ tsp baking soda
- 1 tsp cinnamon
- 1 cup papaya

DIRECTIONS

1. In a bowl combine all wet ingredients
2. In another bowl combine all dry ingredients
3. Combine wet and dry ingredients together
4. Pour mixture into 8-12 prepared muffin cups, fill 2/3 of the cups
5. Bake for 18-20 minutes at 375 F
6. When ready remove from the oven and serve

PLANTAIN MUFFINS

Serves: *8-12*

Prep Time: ***10*** Minutes

Cook Time: ***20*** Minutes

Total Time: ***30*** Minutes

INGREDIENTS

- 2 eggs
- 1 tablespoon olive oil
- 1 cup milk
- 2 cups whole wheat flour
- 1 tsp baking soda
- ¼ tsp baking soda
- 1 tsp cinnamon
- 1 cup plantain

DIRECTIONS

1. In a bowl combine all wet ingredients
2. In another bowl combine all dry ingredients
3. Combine wet and dry ingredients together
4. Pour mixture into 8-12 prepared muffin cups, fill 2/3 of the cups
5. Bake for 18-20 minutes at 375 F
6. When ready remove from the oven and serve

ONION OMELETTE

Serves: *1*

Prep Time: *5* Minutes

Cook Time: *10* Minutes

Total Time: *15* Minutes

INGREDIENTS

- **2 eggs**
- **¼ tsp salt**
- **¼ tsp black pepper**
- **1 tablespoon olive oil**
- **¼ cup cheese**
- **¼ tsp basil**
- **1 cup red onion**

DIRECTIONS

1. **In a bowl combine all ingredients together and mix well**
2. **In a skillet heat olive oil and pour the egg mixture**
3. **Cook for 1-2 minutes per side**
4. **When ready remove omelette from the skillet and serve**

BEETROOT OMELETTE

Serves: *1*

Prep Time: *5* Minutes

Cook Time: *10* Minutes

Total Time: *15* Minutes

INGREDIENTS

- **2 eggs**
- **¼ tsp salt**
- **¼ tsp black pepper**
- **1 tablespoon olive oil**
- **¼ cup cheese**
- **¼ tsp basil**
- **1 cup mushrooms**

DIRECTIONS

1. **In a bowl combine all ingredients together and mix well**
2. **In a skillet heat olive oil and pour the egg mixture**
3. **Cook for 1-2 minutes per side**
4. **When ready remove omelette from the skillet and serve**

BELL PEPPER OMELETTE

Serves: *1*

Prep Time: *5* Minutes

Cook Time: *10* Minutes

Total Time: *15* Minutes

INGREDIENTS

- 2 eggs
- ¼ tsp salt
- ¼ tsp black pepper
- 1 tablespoon olive oil
- ¼ cup cheese
- ¼ tsp basil
- 1 cup yellow bell pepper

DIRECTIONS

1. In a bowl combine all ingredients together and mix well
2. In a skillet heat olive oil and pour the egg mixture
3. Cook for 1-2 minutes per side
4. When ready remove omelette from the skillet and serve

TART RECIPES

PEAR TART

Serves: *6-8*

Prep Time: *25* Minutes

Cook Time: *25* Minutes

Total Time: *50* Minutes

INGREDIENTS

- **1 lb. pears**
- **2 oz. brown sugar**
- **½ lb. flaked almonds**
- **¼ lb. porridge oat**
- **2 oz. flour**
- **¼ lb. almonds**
- **pastry sheets**
- **2 tablespoons syrup**

DIRECTIONS

1. **Preheat oven to 400 F, unfold pastry sheets and place them on a baking sheet**
2. **Toss together all ingredients together and mix well**

3. Spread mixture in a single layer on the pastry sheets
4. Before baking decorate with your desired fruits
5. Bake at 400 F for 22-25 minutes or until golden brown
6. When ready remove from the oven and serve

CARDAMOM TART

Serves: *6-8*

Prep Time: 25 Minutes

Cook Time: 25 Minutes

Total Time: *50* Minutes

INGREDIENTS

- 4-5 pears
- 2 tablespoons lemon juice
- pastry sheets

CARDAMOM FILLING

- ½ lb. butter
- ½ lb. brown sugar
- ½ lb. almonds
- ¼ lb. flour
- 1 ¼ tsp cardamom
- 2 eggs

DIRECTIONS

1. **Preheat oven to 400 F, unfold pastry sheets and place them on a baking sheet**
2. **Toss together all ingredients together and mix well**
3. **Spread mixture in a single layer on the pastry sheets**
4. **Before baking decorate with your desired fruits**

5. **Bake at 400 F for 22-25 minutes or until golden brown**
6. **When ready remove from the oven and serve**

PEACH PECAN PIE

Serves: *8-12*

Prep Time: *15* Minutes

Cook Time: *35* Minutes

Total Time: *50* Minutes

INGREDIENTS

- **4-5 cups peaches**
- **1 tablespoon preserves**
- **1 cup sugar**
- **4 small egg yolks**
- **¼ cup flour**
- **1 tsp vanilla extract**

DIRECTIONS

1. **Line a pie plate or pie form with pastry and cover the edges of the plate depending on your preference**
2. **In a bowl combine all pie ingredients together and mix well**
3. **Pour the mixture over the pastry**
4. **Bake at 400-425 F for 25-30 minutes or until golden brown**
5. **When ready remove from the oven and let it rest for 15 minutes**

BUTTERFINGER PIE

Serves: *8-12*

Prep Time: *15* Minutes

Cook Time: *35* Minutes

Total Time: *50* Minutes

INGREDIENTS

- **pastry sheets**
- **1 package cream cheese**
- **1 tsp vanilla extract**
- **¼ cup peanut butter**
- **1 cup powdered sugar (to decorate)**
- **2 cups Butterfinger candy bars**
- **8 oz whipped topping**

DIRECTIONS

1. **Line a pie plate or pie form with pastry and cover the edges of the plate depending on your preference**
2. **In a bowl combine all pie ingredients together and mix well**
3. **Pour the mixture over the pastry**
4. **Bake at 400-425 F for 25-30 minutes or until golden brown**
5. **When ready remove from the oven and let it rest for 15 minutes**

STRAWBERRY PIE

Serves: *8-12*

Prep Time: *15* Minutes

Cook Time: *35* Minutes

Total Time: *50* Minutes

INGREDIENTS

- pastry sheets
- 1,5 lb. strawberries
- 1 cup powdered sugar
- 2 tablespoons cornstarch
- 1 tablespoon lime juice
- 1 tsp vanilla extract
- 2 eggs
- 2 tablespoons butter

DIRECTIONS

1. Line a pie plate or pie form with pastry and cover the edges of the plate depending on your preference
2. In a bowl combine all pie ingredients together and mix well
3. Pour the mixture over the pastry
4. Bake at 400-425 F for 25-30 minutes or until golden brown
5. When ready remove from the oven and let it rest for 15 minutes

BLUEBERRY PIE

Serves: *8-12*

Prep Time: *15* Minutes

Cook Time: *35* Minutes

Total Time: *50* Minutes

INGREDIENTS

- pastry sheets
- ¼ tsp lavender
- 1 cup brown sugar
- 4-5 cups blueberries
- 1 tablespoon lemon juice
- 1 cup almonds
- 2 tablespoons butter

DIRECTIONS

1. Line a pie plate or pie form with pastry and cover the edges of the plate depending on your preference
2. In a bowl combine all pie ingredients together and mix well
3. Pour the mixture over the pastry
4. Bake at 400-425 F for 25-30 minutes or until golden brown
5. When ready remove from the oven and let it rest for 15 minutes

SMOOTHIE RECIPES

GINGER-OAT SMOOTHIE

Serves: *1*

Prep Time: 5 Minutes

Cook Time: 5 Minutes

Total Time: *10* Minutes

INGREDIENTS

- **½ cup oats**
- **¼ cup blueberries**
- **¼ cup vanilla yogurt**
- **1 cup ice**
- **¼ tsp ginger**

DIRECTIONS

1. **In a blender place all ingredients and blend until smooth**
2. **Pour smoothie in a glass and serve**

PUMPKIN SMOOTHIE

Serves: *1*
Prep Time: *5* Minutes

Cook Time: *5* Minutes

Total Time: *10* Minutes

INGREDIENTS

- **1 cup ice**
- **1 cup almond milk**
- **½ cup pumpkin puree**
- **1 tsp honey**

DIRECTIONS

1. **In a blender place all ingredients and blend until smooth**
2. **Pour smoothie in a glass and serve**

GREEN SMOOTHIE

Serves: ***1***

Prep Time: 5 Minutes

Cook Time: 5 Minutes

Total Time: ***10*** Minutes

INGREDIENTS

- **1 cup kale**
- **1 celery**
- **1 banana**
- **1 cup apple juice**
- **1 cup ice**

DIRECTIONS

1. **In a blender place all ingredients and blend until smooth**
2. **Pour smoothie in a glass and serve**

MANGO SMOOTHIE

Serves: *1*

Prep Time: *5* Minutes

Cook Time: *5* Minutes

Total Time: *10* Minutes

INGREDIENTS

- **1 cup mango**
- **½ cup coconut milk**
- **1 cup ice**
- **½ cup vanilla yogurt**
- **1 tsp honey**

DIRECTIONS

1. **In a blender place all ingredients and blend until smooth**
2. **Pour smoothie in a glass and serve**

PINEAPPLE SMOOTHIE

Serves: *1*

Prep Time: *5* Minutes

Cook Time: *5* Minutes

Total Time: *10* Minutes

INGREDIENTS

- **1 cup pineapple**
- **1 cup ice**
- **1 orange juice**
- **½ cup carrot**
- **1 banana**

DIRECTIONS

1. **In a blender place all ingredients and blend until smooth**
2. **Pour smoothie in a glass and serve**

CASHEW SMOOTHIE

Serves: *1*
Prep Time: *5* Minutes
Cook Time: *5* Minutes
Total Time: *10* Minutes

INGREDIENTS

- 1 cup cashews
- 1 cup ice
- 1 banana
- 1 tablespoon honey

DIRECTIONS

1. **In a blender place all ingredients and blend until smooth**
2. **Pour smoothie in a glass and serve**

NUT SMOOTHIE

Serves: *1*

Prep Time: *5* Minutes

Cook Time: *5* Minutes

Total Time: *10* Minutes

INGREDIENTS

- **1 cup coconut milk**
- **1 cup raspberries**
- **1 banana**
- **1 tablespoon peanut butter**
- **1 tsp agave nectar**

DIRECTIONS

1. **In a blender place all ingredients and blend until smooth**
2. **Pour smoothie in a glass and serve**

STRAWBERRY SMOOTHIE

Serves: *1*

Prep Time: *5* Minutes

Cook Time: *5* Minutes

Total Time: ***10*** Minutes

INGREDIENTS

- **1 cup strawberries**
- **1 cup Greek Yoghurt**
- **½ cup orange juice**
- **1 tsp honey**
- **1 tablespoon flaxseed meal**

DIRECTIONS

1. **In a blender place all ingredients and blend until smooth**
2. **Pour smoothie in a glass and serve**

SPINACH & GRAPE SMOOTHIE

Serves: *1*

Prep Time: 5 Minutes

Cook Time: 5 Minutes

Total Time: *10* Minutes

INGREDIENTS

- 1 cup grapes
- 1 cup baby spinach
- 1 cup ice
- 1 cup almond milk

DIRECTIONS

1. **In a blender place all ingredients and blend until smooth**
2. **Pour smoothie in a glass and serve**

ICE-CREAM RECIPES

SAFFRON ICE-CREAM

Serves: *6-8*

Prep Time: *15* Minutes

Cook Time: *15* Minutes

Total Time: *30* Minutes

INGREDIENTS

- 4 egg yolks
- 1 cup heavy cream
- 1 cup milk
- ½ cup brown sugar
- 1 tsp saffron
- 1 tsp vanilla extract

DIRECTIONS

1. In a saucepan whisk together all ingredients
2. Mix until bubbly
3. Strain into a bowl and cool
4. Whisk in favorite fruits and mix well
5. Cover and refrigerate for 2-3 hours

6. **Pour mixture in the ice-cream maker and follow manufacturer instructions**
7. **Serve when ready**

PISTACHIOS ICE-CREAM

Serves: *6-8*

Prep Time: *15* Minutes

Cook Time: *15* Minutes

Total Time: *30* Minutes

INGREDIENTS

- 4 egg yolks
- 1 cup heavy cream
- 1 cup milk
- 1 cup sugar
- 1 vanilla bean
- 1 tsp almond extract
- 1 cup cherries
- ½ cup pistachios

DIRECTIONS

1. In a saucepan whisk together all ingredients
2. Mix until bubbly
3. Strain into a bowl and cool
4. Whisk in favorite fruits and mix well
5. Cover and refrigerate for 2-3 hours
6. Pour mixture in the ice-cream maker and follow manufacturer instructions

VANILLA ICE-CREAM

Serves: *6-8*

Prep Time: ***15*** Minutes

Cook Time: ***15*** Minutes

Total Time: ***30*** Minutes

INGREDIENTS

- **1 cup milk**
- **1 tablespoon cornstarch**
- **1 oz. cream cheese**
- **1 cup heavy cream**
- **1 cup brown sugar**
- **1 tablespoon corn syrup**
- **1 vanilla bean**

DIRECTIONS

1. **In a saucepan whisk together all ingredients**
2. **Mix until bubbly**
3. **Strain into a bowl and cool**
4. **Whisk in favorite fruits and mix well**
5. **Cover and refrigerate for 2-3 hours**
6. **Pour mixture in the ice-cream maker and follow manufacturer instructions**
7. **Serve when ready**

THIRD COOKBOOK

SPICY SHRIMP STIR FRY

Serves: *1*
Prep Time: *10* Minutes

Cook Time: *10* Minutes

Total Time: *20* Minutes

INGREDIENTS

- 1 orange
- Cayenne powder
- 3 oz shrimp
- Ginger powder
- 4 tbs vegetable stock
- Curry powder
- 25 cups red onion
- 1 cup cabbage
- Garlic powder

DIRECTIONS

1. Coat the shrimp in the seasonings.
2. Pour the broth into a pan, then add cabbage, onion, and shrimp.
3. Cook until the shrimp turns pink.
4. Serve topped with orange juice and orange slices.

ARTICHOKE AND SPINACH PIZZA

Serves: *6-8*

Prep Time: ***10*** Minutes

Cook Time: *15* Minutes

Total Time: *25* Minutes

INGREDIENTS

- **1 pizza crust**
- **1 garlic clove**
- **½ lb. spinach**
- **½ lb. soft cheese**
- **2 oz. artichoke hearts**
- **1 cup mozzarella cheese**
- **1 tablespoon olive oil**

DIRECTIONS

1. **Spread tomato sauce on the pizza crust**
2. **Place all the toppings on the pizza crust**
3. **Bake the pizza at 425 F for 12-15 minutes**
4. **When ready remove pizza from the oven and serve**

MINT PIZZA

Serves: *6-8*

Prep Time: *10* Minutes

Cook Time: *15* Minutes

Total Time: *25* Minutes

INGREDIENTS

- 1 pizza crust
- 1 olive oil
- 1 garlic clove
- 1 cup mozzarella cheese
- 2 oz. mint
- 2 courgettes

DIRECTIONS

1. Spread tomato sauce on the pizza crust
2. Place all the toppings on the pizza crust
3. Bake the pizza at 425 F for 12-15 minutes
4. When ready remove pizza from the oven and serve

SAUSAGE PIZZA

Serves: *6-8*

Prep Time: *10* Minutes

Cook Time: *15* Minutes

Total Time: 25 Minutes

INGREDIENTS

- 2 pork sausages
- 1 tablespoon olive oil
- 2 garlic cloves
- 1 tsp fennel seeds
- ½ lb. ricotta
- 1 cup mozzarella cheese
- 1 oz. parmesan cheese
- 1 pizza crust

DIRECTIONS

1. Spread tomato sauce on the pizza crust
2. Place all the toppings on the pizza crust
3. Bake the pizza at 425 F for 12-15 minutes
4. When ready remove pizza from the oven and serve

BEEF & BROCCOLI STIR FRY

Serves: ***4***

Prep Time: ***10*** Minutes

Cook Time: ***30*** Minutes

Total Time: ***40*** Minutes

INGREDIENTS

- **2 cloves garlic**
- **½ lb Beef Sirloin steaks**
- **Chicken broth**
- **2 tbs liquid Aminos**
- **1 tsp onion powder**
- **1 tbs parsley**
- **2 cups broccoli florets**

DIRECTIONS

1. **Sauté the beef in a few tbs of chicken broth until brown.**
2. **Add onion powder, garlic, broccoli, liquid aminos and parsley.**
3. **Saute until well done.**
4. **Serve immediately.**

GINGER CHICKEN SOUP

Serves: *1*

Prep Time: *5* Minutes

Cook Time: *15* Minutes

Total Time: *20* Minutes

INGREDIENTS

- 2 cloves garlic
- Salt
- Pepper
- 3 stalks celery
- 3 oz chicken tenders
- 4 cups chicken broth
- 4 slices ginger

DIRECTIONS

1. **Bring the broth to a boil.**
2. **Add the garlic, ginger, and celery.**
3. **Simmer for 5 minutes.**
4. **Add in the chicken and boil for 10 more minutes.**
5. **Season with salt and pepper.**
6. **Serve immediately.**

CILANTRO SKEWERS

Serves: *1*

Prep Time: *20* Minutes

Cook Time: *120* Minutes

Total Time: *140* Minutes

INGREDIENTS

- Cherry tomatoes
- Red pepper flakes
- Salt
- Pepper
- 2 tbs lemon juice
- Cilantro
- 100g shrimp

DIRECTIONS

1. **Mix the cilantro, red pepper flakes, salt, pepper and shrimp together.**
2. **Marinade for at least 2 hours.**
3. **Place on skewers alternating with tomatoes.**
4. **Cook on a barbeque.**
5. **Season with salt and pepper.**
6. **Serve immediately.**

CURRY SHRIMP

Serves: *14*
Prep Time: *10* Minutes

Cook Time: *10* Minutes

Total Time: *20* Minutes

INGREDIENTS

- 1/8 cup water
- 100g shrimp
- 1 onion
- Pepper
- 1/ tsp curry powder
- ¼ tsp cumin
- Salt
- 4 garlic cloves

DIRECTIONS

1. Cook the garlic and onion until translucent.
2. Add in the shrimp, seasonings and water.
3. Cook until done.
4. Serve immediately.

ORANGE ROUGHY

Serves: *1*

Prep Time: *10* Minutes

Cook Time: *15* Minutes

Total Time: 25 Minutes

INGREDIENTS

- **100g orange roughy fillet**
- **2 tbs lemon juice**
- **1 tsp thyme**
- **1 tsp rosemary**
- **¼ tsp onion powder**
- **Salt**
- **Pepper**

DIRECTIONS

1. **Place the ingredients in a baking dish and cover with tin foil.**
2. **Bake at 350F for 15 minutes.**
3. **Serve hot.**

LEMON TILAPIA

Serves: *1*

Prep Time: *10* Minutes

Cook Time: *20* Minutes

Total Time: *30* Minutes

INGREDIENTS

- ¼ cup lemon juice
- 1 lemon zest
- 100g tilapia
- 1 tbs onion
- 1 tsp dill
- Salt
- Pepper

DIRECTIONS

1. Place the ingredients in a tin foil, then wrap them up.
2. Cook on a grill until done
3. Serve when ready

MEDITERRANEAN SEA BASS

Serves: *1*

Prep Time: *10* Minutes

Cook Time: *10* Minutes

Total Time: *20* Minutes

INGREDIENTS

- **100g sea Bass**
- **2 cloves garlic**
- **1 lemon juice**
- **1 lemon zest**
- **1 tbs onion**
- **½ tsp parsley**
- **Salt**
- **Pepper**

DIRECTIONS

1. **Place the ingredients in a tin foil bag.**
2. **Cook on the barbeque for 10 minutes.**
3. **Serve topped with fresh parsley.**

WASABI WHITEFISH

Serves: *1*

Prep Time: *10* Minutes

Cook Time: *5* Minutes

Total Time: *15* Minutes

INGREDIENTS

- **½ tsp ginger**
- **100g whitefish**
- **1 tbs mustard**
- **1 tsp wasabi powder**

DIRECTIONS

1. **Mix the mustard with the wasabi powder.**
2. **Add the ginger.**
3. **Coat the fish with the mixture.**
4. **Allow to sit for at least half an hour.**
5. **Grill for 5 minutes.**
6. **Serve hot.**

CAJUN CHICKEN

Serves: *1*

Prep Time: *5* Minutes

Cook Time: *25* Minutes

Total Time: ***30*** Minutes

INGREDIENTS

- **½ tbs milk**
- **½ tsp Cajun seasoning**
- **100g chicken**

DIRECTIONS

1. **Preheat the oven to 350F.**
2. **Coat the chicken with milk.**
3. **Sprinkle with Cajun seasoning.**
4. **Bake for 25 minutes.**
5. **Serve immediately.**

Serves: *1*

Prep Time: *5* Minutes

Cook Time: *0* Minutes

Total Time: *5* Minutes

INGREDIENTS

- **½ tomato**
- **1 toast**
- **100g chicken**
- **Basil**
- **Salt**
- **Pepper**

DIRECTIONS

1. **Cook the chicken, allow to chill, then shred.**
2. **Arrange the ingredients on top of the toast.**
3. **Serve immediately.**

MARINARA CHICKEN

Serves: *1*

Prep Time: *10* Minutes

Cook Time: 25 Minutes

Total Time: 35 Minutes

INGREDIENTS

- ½ tsp oregano
- Parsley
- 100g chicken
- 1 toast
- ½ tsp basil
- 3 garlic cloves
- 2 tsp onion
- Salt
- Pepper

DIRECTIONS

1. **Crush the toast and combine with oregano, basil, salt, and pepper.**
2. **Coat the chicken with the mixture and place in a casserole dish.**
3. **Cook covered for 25 minutes at 375F.**
4. **Serve topped with marinara sauce and parsley.**

EDAMAME FRITATTA

Serves: 2
Prep Time: *10* Minutes

Cook Time: *20* Minutes

Total Time: *30* Minutes

INGREDIENTS

- 1 cup edamame
- 1 tablespoon olive oil
- ½ red onion
- 2 eggs
- ¼ tsp salt
- 2 oz. cheddar cheese
- 1 garlic clove
- ¼ tsp dill

DIRECTIONS

1. In a bowl whisk eggs with salt and cheese
2. In a frying pan heat olive oil and pour egg mixture
3. Add remaining ingredients and mix well
4. Serve when ready

LEEKS FRITATTA

Serves: *2*

Prep Time: *10* Minutes

Cook Time: *20* Minutes

Total Time: *30* Minutes

INGREDIENTS

- ½ lb. leek
- 1 tablespoon olive oil
- ½ red onion
- ¼ tsp salt
- 2 eggs
- 2 oz. cheddar cheese
- 1 garlic clove
- ¼ tsp dill

DIRECTIONS

1. In a bowl whisk eggs with salt and cheese
2. In a frying pan heat olive oil and pour egg mixture
3. Add remaining ingredients and mix well
4. Serve when ready

MUSHROOM FRITATTA

Serves: 2

Prep Time: *10* Minutes

Cook Time: *20* Minutes

Total Time: *30* Minutes

INGREDIENTS

- ½ lb. mushrooms
- 1 tablespoon olive oil
- ½ red onion
- ¼ tsp salt
- 2 eggs
- 2 oz. cheddar cheese
- 1 garlic clove
- ¼ tsp dill

DIRECTIONS

1. In a bowl whisk eggs with salt and cheese
2. In a frying pan heat olive oil and pour egg mixture
3. Add remaining ingredients and mix well
4. Serve when ready

PEAS FRITATTA

Serves: *2*

Prep Time: *10* Minutes

Cook Time: *20* Minutes

Total Time: *30* Minutes

INGREDIENTS

- **1 cup peas**
- **1 tablespoon olive oil**
- **½ red onion**
- **¼ tsp salt**
- **2 eggs**
- **2 oz. cheddar cheese**
- **1 garlic clove**
- **¼ tsp dill**

DIRECTIONS

1. **In a bowl whisk eggs with salt and cheese**
2. **In a frying pan heat olive oil and pour egg mixture**
3. **Add remaining ingredients and mix well**
4. **Serve when ready.**

BELL PEPPER FRITATTA

Serves: 2

Prep Time: *10* Minutes

Cook Time: *20* Minutes

Total Time: *30* Minutes

INGREDIENTS

- 1 cup red bell pepper
- 1 tablespoon olive oil
- ½ red onion
- ¼ tsp salt
- 2 eggs
- 2 oz. parmesan cheese
- 1 garlic clove
- ¼ tsp dill

DIRECTIONS

1. In a bowl whisk eggs with salt and cheese
2. In a frying pan heat olive oil and pour egg mixture
3. Add remaining ingredients and mix well
4. Serve when ready.

POTATO FRITATTA

Serves: 2
Prep Time: *10* Minutes

Cook Time: *20* Minutes

Total Time: *30* Minutes

INGREDIENTS

- 1 cup sweet potato
- 1 tablespoon olive oil
- ½ red onion
- ¼ tsp salt
- 2 eggs
- 2 oz. cheddar cheese
- 1 garlic clove
- ¼ tsp dill

DIRECTIONS

1. **In a bowl whisk eggs with salt and cheese**
2. **In a frying pan heat olive oil and pour egg mixture**
3. **Add remaining ingredients and mix well**
4. **Serve when ready**

SKILLET PIZZA

Serves: *1*

Prep Time: *10* Minutes

Cook Time: *20* Minutes

Total Time: *30* Minutes

INGREDIENTS

- ¼ red onion
- ½ cup red bell pepper
- ¼ tsp salt
- 2 eggs
- 1 cup tomato sauce
- 1 cup mozzarella cheese
- 1 pizza crust

DIRECTIONS

1. On a pizza crust spread tomato sauce
2. Add toppings on pizza
3. Place pizza in the skillet and cover with a lid
4. Cook on low heat for 18-20 minutes or until pizza is ready

GLAZED PORK CHOPS

Serves: ***4***

Prep Time: ***10*** Minutes

Cook Time: ***15*** Minutes

Total Time: ***25*** Minutes

INGREDIENTS

- **1 cup all-purpose flour**
- **4 pork loin chops**
- **½ cup maple syrup**
- **1 tablespoon cornstarch**
- **1 cup brown sugar**
- **pinch of salt**
- **2 tablespoons water**

DIRECTIONS

1. **In a bowl combine salt and flour together**
2. **Place the pork chops in the bowl and turn to coat**
3. **Place pork chops in a skillet and cook until golden brown**
4. **Add maple syrup, sugar, water cornstarch, and bring to a boil**
5. **Cook until the sugar is dissolved and meat is cooked**
6. **When ready remove from the skillet and serve**

PANINI CHICKEN

Serves: *1*

Prep Time: *10* Minutes

Cook Time: *15* Minutes

Total Time: *25* Minutes

INGREDIENTS

- **1 lb. chicken breast**
- **1 tsp gingerroot**
- **½ cup chicken broth**
- **¼ tsp salt**
- **¼ tsp turmeric**
- **4 green onion**

DIRECTIONS

1. **In a slow cooker place your chicken and add broth, garlic clove, green onions and gingerroot**
2. **When ready remove chicken mixture and place the chicken on a flatbread**
3. **Cook sandwich in a panini maker**
4. **When ready remove and serve**

PENNE PASTA

Serves: 2

Prep Time: *10* Minutes

Cook Time: *20* Minutes

Total Time: *30* Minutes

INGREDIENTS

- 1 package penne pasta
- 1 onion
- 1 tablespoon thyme
- 1 tablespoon basil
- ¼ cup white wine
- 1 tablespoon tomato paste
- 1 tablespoon all-purpose flour
- 1 cup parmesan cheese

DIRECTIONS

1. In a stockpot cook pasta al dente
2. In a skillet sauté onion until soft, add salt, herbs, tomato paste, flour and cook for 2-3 minutes
3. Add pasta to the tomato mixture and bring to a boil
4. When ready serve with parmesan cheese on top

TURKEY SANDWICH

Serves:	*1*	
Prep Time:	*5*	Minutes
Cook Time:	*5*	Minutes
Total Time:	*10*	Minutes

INGREDIENTS

- 2 oz. cream cheese
- 2 tablespoons salad dressing
- 1 tsp garlic powder
- 1 loaf bread
- Lettuce
- 1 lb. cooked turkey
- ½ lb. swiss cheese
- 1 tomato

DIRECTIONS

1. In a bowl combine cream cheese, garlic powder and salad dressing
2. Spread mixture on the bread
3. Add lettuce, tomatoes, cheese and turkey
4. Serve when ready

ROASTED SQUASH

Serves: *3-4*

Prep Time: *10* Minutes

Cook Time: *20* Minutes

Total Time: *30* Minutes

INGREDIENTS

- 2 delicata squashes
- 2 tablespoons olive oil
- 1 tsp curry powder
- 1 tsp salt

DIRECTIONS

1. Preheat the oven to 400 F
2. Cut everything in half lengthwise
3. Toss everything with olive oil and place onto a prepared baking sheet
4. Roast for 18-20 minutes at 400 F or until golden brown
5. When ready remove from the oven and serve

BRUSSELS SPROUT CHIPS

Serves: 2

Prep Time: *10* Minutes

Cook Time: *20* Minutes

Total Time: *30* Minutes

INGREDIENTS

- **1 lb. brussels sprouts**
- **1 tablespoon olive oil**
- **1 tablespoon parmesan cheese**
- **1 tsp garlic powder**
- **1 tsp seasoning**

DIRECTIONS

1. **Preheat the oven to 425 F**
2. **In a bowl toss everything with olive oil and seasoning**
3. **Spread everything onto a prepared baking sheet**
4. **Bake for 8-10 minutes or until crisp**
5. **When ready remove from the oven and serve**

BEET CHIPS

Serves: 2

Prep Time: *10* Minutes

Cook Time: *20* Minutes

Total Time: *30* Minutes

INGREDIENTS

- 1 lb. beet
- 1 tablespoon olive oil
- 1 tablespoon parmesan cheese
- 1 tsp garlic powder
- 1 tsp seasoning

DIRECTIONS

1. Preheat the oven to 425 F
2. In a bowl toss everything with olive oil and seasoning
3. Spread everything onto a prepared baking sheet
4. Bake for 8-10 minutes or until crisp
5. When ready remove from the oven and serve

SPINACH CHIPS

Serves: 2

Prep Time: *10* Minutes

Cook Time: *20* Minutes

Total Time: *30* Minutes

INGREDIENTS

- 1 lb. spinach
- 1 tablespoon olive oil
- 1 tablespoon parmesan cheese
- 1 tsp garlic powder
- 1 tsp seasoning

DIRECTIONS

1. Preheat the oven to 425 F
2. In a bowl toss everything with olive oil and seasoning
3. Spread everything onto a prepared baking sheet
4. Bake for 8-10 minutes or until crisp
5. When ready remove from the oven and serve

KALE CHIPS

Serves: 2

Prep Time: *10* Minutes

Cook Time: *20* Minutes

Total Time: *30* Minutes

INGREDIENTS

- 1 lb. kale
- 1 tablespoon olive oil
- 1 tablespoon parmesan cheese
- 1 tsp garlic powder
- 1 tsp seasoning

DIRECTIONS

1. Preheat the oven to 425 F
2. In a bowl toss everything with olive oil and seasoning
3. Spread everything onto a prepared baking sheet
4. Bake for 8-10 minutes or until crisp
5. When ready remove from the oven and serve

EGGPLANT CHIPS

Serves: 2

Prep Time: *10* Minutes

Cook Time: *20* Minutes

Total Time: *30* Minutes

INGREDIENTS

- **1 lb. eggplant**
- **1 tablespoon olive oil**
- **1 tablespoon parmesan cheese**
- **1 tsp garlic powder**
- **1 tsp seasoning**

DIRECTIONS

1. **Preheat the oven to 425 F**
2. **In a bowl toss everything with olive oil and seasoning**
3. **Spread everything onto a prepared baking sheet**
4. **Bake for 8-10 minutes or until crisp**
5. **When ready remove from the oven and serve**

TOMATO CHIPS

Serves: 2

Prep Time: *10* Minutes

Cook Time: *20* Minutes

Total Time: *30* Minutes

INGREDIENTS

- **1 lb. tomato**
- **1 tablespoon olive oil**
- **1 tablespoon parmesan cheese**
- **1 tsp garlic powder**
- **1 tsp seasoning**

DIRECTIONS

1. **Preheat the oven to 425 F**
2. **In a bowl toss everything with olive oil and seasoning**
3. **Spread everything onto a prepared baking sheet**
4. **Bake for 8-10 minutes or until crisp**
5. **When ready remove from the oven and serve**

PASTA

SIMPLE SPAGHETTI

Serves: 2
Prep Time: 5 Minutes

Cook Time: *15* Minutes

Total Time: *20* Minutes

INGREDIENTS

- 10 oz. spaghetti
- 2 eggs
- ½ cup parmesan cheese
- 1 tsp black pepper
- Olive oil
- 1 tsp parsley
- 2 cloves garlic

DIRECTIONS

1. **In a pot boil spaghetti (or any other type of pasta), drain and set aside**
2. **In a bowl whish eggs with parmesan cheese**
3. **In a skillet heat olive oil, add garlic and cook for 1-2 minutes**
4. **Pour egg mixture and mix well**
5. **Add pasta and stir well**

6. **When ready garnish with parsley and serve**

COUSCOUS SALAD

Serves: *5*

Prep Time: *10* Minutes

Cook Time: *50* Minutes

Total Time: *60* Minutes

INGREDIENTS

Salad

- Spinach leaves
- Seasonings
- ½ pumpkin
- 1 cup cous cous
- 2 chicken breasts

Dressing

- 2 tbs vinegar
- 3 tbs olive oil
- 2 tbs mustard
- 4 tbs mayonnaise
- 2 tbs lemon juice
- Pepper
- Salt

DIRECTIONS

1. **Peel and cut the pumpkin**
2. **Toss in oil and season**
3. **Roast in oven for at least 30 minutes**
4. **Grill the chicken**
5. **Cook the cous cous**
6. **Mix the dressing ingredients together**
7. **Mix everyting together in a salad bowl**
8. **Serve**

POTATO SALAD

Serves: 2

Prep Time: 5 Minutes

Cook Time: *10* Minutes

Total Time: *15* Minutes

INGREDIENTS

- **5 potatoes**
- **1 tsp cumin seeds**
- **1/3 cup oil**
- **2 tsp mustard**
- **1 red onion**
- **2 cloves garlic**
- **1/3 cup lemon juice**
- **1 tsp sea salt**

DIRECTIONS

1. **Steam the potatoes until tender**
2. **Mix mustard, turmeric powder, lemon juice, cumin seeds, and salt**
3. **Place the potatoes in a bowl and pour the lemon mixture over**
4. **Add the chopped onion and minced garlic over**
5. **Stir to coat and refrigerate covered**
6. **Add oil and stir before serving**

CARROT SALAD

Serves: 2

Prep Time: *5* Minutes

Cook Time: *5* Minutes

Total Time: ***10*** Minutes

INGREDIENTS

- 1 ½ tbs lemon juice
- 1/3 tsp salt
- ¼ tsp black pepper
- 2 tbs olive oil
- 1/3 lb carrots
- 1 tsp mustard

DIRECTIONS

1. **Mix mustard, lemon juice and oil together**
2. **Peel and shred the carrots in a bowl**
3. **Stir in the dressing and season with salt and pepper**
4. **Mix well and allow to chill for at least 30 minutes**
5. **Serve**

MOROCCAN SALAD

Serves: 2

Prep Time: *5* Minutes

Cook Time: *5* Minutes

Total Time: ***10*** Minutes

INGREDIENTS

- 2 tbs lemon juice
- 1 tsp cumin
- 1 tsp paprika
- 3 tbs olive oil
- 2 cloves garlic
- 5 carrots
- Salt
- Pepper

DIRECTIONS

1. **Peel and slice the carrots**
2. **Add the carrots in boiled water and simmer for at least 5 minute**
3. **Drain and rinse the carrots under cold water**
4. **Add in a bowl**
5. **Mix the lemon juice, garlic, cumin, paprika, and olive oil together**

6. **Pour the mixture over the carrots and toss then season with salt and pepper**
7. **Serve immediately**

AVOCADO CHICKEN SALAD

Serves: 2

Prep Time: 5 Minutes

Cook Time: 5 Minutes

Total Time: *10* Minutes

INGREDIENTS

- 3 tsp lime juice
- 3 tbs cilantro
- 1 chicken breast
- 1 avocado
- 1/3 cup onion
- 1 apple
- 1 cup celery
- Salt
- Pepper
- Olive oil

DIRECTIONS

1. Dice the chicken breast
2. Season with salt and pepper and cook into a greased skillet unti golden
3. Dice the vegetables and place over the chicken in a bowl
4. Mash the avocado and sprinkle in the cilantro

5. **Season with salt and pepper and add lime juice**
6. **Serve drizzled with olive oil**

CUCUMBER SALAD

Serves: *8*

Prep Time: 5 Minutes

Cook Time: 5 Minutes

Total Time: ***10*** Minutes

INGREDIENTS

- **2 cucumbers**
- **½ cup vinegar**
- **2 tsp sugar**
- **1/3 cup water**
- **2 tbs sour cream**
- **½ tbs salt**
- **1 ½ tsp paprika**
- **½ onion**

DIRECTIONS

1. **Peel and slice the cucumbers**
2. **Place the cucumbers on a baking sheet and sprinkle with salt**
3. **Allow to chill for about 30 minutes then squeeze out the excess water**
4. **Place the onion slices in a bowl and add the drained cucumbers over**
5. **Add water, sugar, vinegar and paprika**

6. **Allow to marinate for at least 2 hours**
7. **Serve**

MANGO SALAD

Serves: ***4***

Prep Time: ***10*** Minutes

Cook Time: ***5*** Minutes

Total Time: ***15*** Minutes

INGREDIENTS

Salad

- **Salad leaves**
- **2 chicken breasts**
- **2 mangoes**
- **2 avocados**
- **2 tbs pine nuts**

Dressing

- **3 tbs oil**
- **Salt**
- **Pepper**
- **2 tbs lemon juice**
- **3 tbs orange juice**
- **1 tsp mustard**

DIRECTIONS

1. **Divide the salat onto 4 plates**
2. **Slice the peeled mango and place over the salad**
3. **Peel and slice the avocado then place it on top**

4. **Grill the chicken, dice it and place it over**
5. **Mix the dressing ingredients together and pour over**
6. **Serve immediately**

RICE SALAD

Serves: *4*

Prep Time: *10* Minutes

Cook Time: *5* Minutes

Total Time: *15* Minutes

INGREDIENTS

Salad

- **3 tbs basil leaves**
- **100g Kalamata olives**
- **3 tbs pine nuts**
- **2 green shallots**
- **½ sun dried tomato**
- **1 cup rice**

Dressing

- **3 tbs oil**
- **Pepper**
- **2 tbs mustard**
- **3 tbs lemon juice**
- **Salt**
- **1 clove garlic**

DIRECTIONS

1. **Cook the rice**
2. **Mix the dressing ingredients together**

3. **Mix the salad ingredients with the rice in a bowl**
4. **Add the dressing and serve**

FOURTH COOKBOOK

PRUNES PANCAKES

Serves: *4*
Prep Time: *10* Minutes

Cook Time: *30* Minutes

Total Time: *40* Minutes

INGREDIENTS

- **1 cup whole wheat flour**
- **¼ tsp baking soda**
- **¼ tsp baking powder**
- **2 eggs**
- **1 cup milk**
- **½ cup prunes**

DIRECTIONS

1. **In a bowl combine all ingredients together and mix well**
2. **In a skillet heat olive oil**
3. **Pour ¼ of the batter and cook each pancake for 1-2 minutes per side**
4. **When ready remove from heat and serve**

PRUNES MUFFINS

Serves: *8-12*

Prep Time: *10* Minutes

Cook Time: *20* Minutes

Total Time: *30* Minutes

INGREDIENTS

- 2 eggs
- 1 tablespoon olive oil
- 1 cup milk
- 2 cups whole wheat flour
- 1 tsp baking soda
- ¼ tsp baking soda
- 1 cup prunes
- 1 tsp cinnamon
- ¼ cup molasses

DIRECTIONS

1. In a bowl combine all wet ingredients
2. In another bowl combine all dry ingredients
3. Combine wet and dry ingredients together
4. Pour mixture into 8-12 prepared muffin cups, fill 2/3 of the cups
5. Bake for 18-20 minutes at 375 F

PLANTAIN MUFFINS

Serves: *8-12*

Prep Time: ***10*** Minutes

Cook Time: ***20*** Minutes

Total Time: ***30*** Minutes

INGREDIENTS

- **2 eggs**
- **1 tablespoon olive oil**
- **1 cup milk**
- **2 cups whole wheat flour**
- **1 tsp baking soda**
- **¼ tsp baking soda**
- **1 tsp cinnamon**
- **1 cup plantain**

DIRECTIONS

1. **In a bowl combine all wet ingredients**
2. **In another bowl combine all dry ingredients**
3. **Combine wet and dry ingredients together**
4. **Pour mixture into 8-12 prepared muffin cups, fill 2/3 of the cups**
5. **Bake for 18-20 minutes at 375 F**
6. **When ready remove from the oven and serve**

BLUEBERRY MUFFINS

Serves: *8-12*

Prep Time: *10* Minutes

Cook Time: *20* Minutes

Total Time: *30* Minutes

INGREDIENTS

- **2 eggs**
- **1 tablespoon olive oil**
- **1 cup milk**
- **2 cups whole wheat flour**
- **1 tsp baking soda**
- **¼ tsp baking soda**
- **1 tsp cinnamon**
- **1 cup blueberries**

DIRECTIONS

1. **In a bowl combine all wet ingredients**
2. **In another bowl combine all dry ingredients**
3. **Combine wet and dry ingredients together**
4. **Fold in blueberries and mix well**
5. **Pour mixture into 8-12 prepared muffin cups, fill 2/3 of the cups**
6. **Bake for 18-20 minutes at 375 F**

PUMPKIN MUFFINS

Serves: *8-12*

Prep Time: ***10*** Minutes

Cook Time: ***20*** Minutes

Total Time: ***30*** Minutes

INGREDIENTS

- **2 eggs**
- **1 tablespoon olive oil**
- **1 cup milk**
- **2 cups whole wheat flour**
- **1 tsp baking soda**
- **¼ tsp baking soda**
- **1 tsp cinnamon**
- **1 cup pumpkin puree**

DIRECTIONS

1. **In a bowl combine all wet ingredients**
2. **In another bowl combine all dry ingredients**
3. **Combine wet and dry ingredients together**
4. **Pour mixture into 8-12 prepared muffin cups, fill 2/3 of the cups**
5. **Bake for 18-20 minutes at 375 F**
6. **When ready remove from the oven and serve**

CHOCOLATE MUFFINS

Serves: *8-12*
Prep Time: ***10*** Minutes

Cook Time: ***20*** Minutes

Total Time: ***30*** Minutes

INGREDIENTS

- **2 eggs**
- **1 tablespoon olive oil**
- **1 cup milk**
- **2 cups whole wheat flour**
- **1 tsp baking soda**
- **¼ tsp baking soda**
- **1 tsp cinnamon**
- **1 cup chocolate chips**

DIRECTIONS

1. **In a bowl combine all wet ingredients**
2. **In another bowl combine all dry ingredients**
3. **Combine wet and dry ingredients together**
4. **Fold in chocolate chips and mix well**
5. **Pour mixture into 8-12 prepared muffin cups, fill 2/3 of the cups**
6. **Bake for 18-20 minutes at 375 F**

GOOSEBERRY MUFFINS

Serves: *8-12*

Prep Time: ***10*** Minutes

Cook Time: ***20*** Minutes

Total Time: ***30*** Minutes

INGREDIENTS

- **2 eggs**
- **1 tablespoon olive oil**
- **1 cup milk**
- **2 cups whole wheat flour**
- **1 tsp baking soda**
- **¼ tsp baking soda**
- **1 tsp gooseberries**

DIRECTIONS

1. **In a bowl combine all wet ingredients**
2. **In another bowl combine all dry ingredients**
3. **Combine wet and dry ingredients together**
4. **Pour mixture into 8-12 prepared muffin cups, fill 2/3 of the cups**
5. **Bake for 18-20 minutes at 375 F**
6. **When ready remove from the oven and serve**

GOAT CHEESE OMELETTE

Serves: *1*

Prep Time: *5* Minutes

Cook Time: *10* Minutes

Total Time: *15* Minutes

INGREDIENTS

- **2 eggs**
- **¼ tsp salt**
- **¼ tsp black pepper**
- **1 tablespoon olive oil**
- **¼ cup goat cheese**
- **¼ tsp basil**

DIRECTIONS

1. **In a bowl combine all ingredients together and mix well**
2. **In a skillet heat olive oil and pour the egg mixture**
3. **Cook for 1-2 minutes per side**
4. **When ready remove omelette from the skillet and serve**

ZUCCHINI OMELETTE

Serves: *1*

Prep Time: *5* Minutes

Cook Time: *10* Minutes

Total Time: *15* Minutes

INGREDIENTS

- **2 eggs**
- **¼ tsp salt**
- **¼ tsp black pepper**
- **1 tablespoon olive oil**
- **¼ cup cheese**
- **¼ tsp basil**
- **1 cup zucchini**

DIRECTIONS

1. **In a bowl combine all ingredients together and mix well**
2. **In a skillet heat olive oil and pour the egg mixture**
3. **Cook for 1-2 minutes per side**
4. **When ready remove omelette from the skillet and serve**

ENCHILADA OMELETTE

Serves: *1*

Prep Time: *5* Minutes

Cook Time: *10* Minutes

Total Time: *15* Minutes

INGREDIENTS

- **2 eggs**
- **¼ tsp salt**
- **¼ tsp black pepper**
- **1 tablespoon olive oil**
- **¼ cup cheese**
- **¼ tsp basil**
- **1 cup enchilada**

DIRECTIONS

1. **In a bowl combine all ingredients together and mix well**
2. **In a skillet heat olive oil and pour the egg mixture**
3. **Cook for 1-2 minutes per side**
4. **When ready remove omelette from the skillet and serve**

RED ONION OMELETTE

Serves: *1*

Prep Time: *5* Minutes

Cook Time: *10* Minutes

Total Time: *15* Minutes

INGREDIENTS

- **2 eggs**
- **¼ tsp salt**
- **¼ tsp black pepper**
- **1 tablespoon olive oil**
- **¼ cup cheese**
- **¼ tsp basil**
- **1 cup red onion**

DIRECTIONS

1. **In a bowl combine all ingredients together and mix well**
2. **In a skillet heat olive oil and pour the egg mixture**
3. **Cook for 1-2 minutes per side**
4. **When ready remove omelette from the skillet and serve**

TOMATO OMELETTE

Serves: *1*

Prep Time: *5* Minutes

Cook Time: *10* Minutes

Total Time: *15* Minutes

INGREDIENTS

- 2 eggs
- ¼ tsp salt
- ¼ tsp black pepper
- 1 tablespoon olive oil
- ¼ cup cheese
- ¼ tsp basil
- 1 cup tomatoes

DIRECTIONS

1. In a bowl combine all ingredients together and mix well
2. In a skillet heat olive oil and pour the egg mixture
3. Cook for 1-2 minutes per side
4. When ready remove omelette from the skillet and serve

BLUEBERRIES GRANOLA

Serves: 2

Prep Time: *10* Minutes

Cook Time: *40* Minutes

Total Time: *50* Minutes

INGREDIENTS

- 1 cup blueberries
- 2 cup porridge oats
- 2 oz. coconut flakes
- 2 oz. brown sugar
- 2 tablespoons honey
- 1/2 cup raisins
- 1 cup chocolate chips

DIRECTIONS

1. In a bowl combine all ingredients together and mix well
2. Spread mixture on a baking sheet
3. Bake at 275 F for 30-40 minutes
4. When ready remove from the oven, cut into bars and serve

CARROT CAKE GRANOLA

Serves: **4-6**

Prep Time: ***10*** Minutes

Cook Time: ***40*** Minutes

Total Time: ***50*** Minutes

INGREDIENTS

- 1 cup oats
- 1 tsp mixed spice
- ¼ lb. walnuts
- 2 carrots
- 2 oz. coconut oil
- 2 oz. honey

DIRECTIONS

1. In a bowl combine all ingredients together and mix well
2. Place the mixture into a baking dish
3. Bake at 350 F for 30-40 minutes
4. When ready remove from the oven and serve

CINNAMON GRANOLA BARS

Serves: *6-8*

Prep Time: ***10*** Minutes

Cook Time: ***40*** Minutes

Total Time: ***50*** Minutes

INGREDIENTS

- ¼ lb. butter
- 2 cups oats
- ¼ lb. sunflower seeds
- 2 oz. sesame seeds
- 2 oz. walnuts
- 2 tablespoons honey
- 1 tsp cinnamon
- 1 cup cherries
- 1 cup blueberries

DIRECTIONS

1. **In a bowl combine all ingredients together and mix well**
2. **Place the mixture into a baking dish**
3. **Bake at 350 F for 30-40 minutes**
4. **When ready remove from the oven cut into bars and serve**

ORANGE GRANOLA

Serves: *6-8*

Prep Time: ***10*** Minutes

Cook Time: ***35*** Minutes

Total Time: ***45*** Minutes

INGREDIENTS

- 1 lb. oats
- Juice from 1 orange
- 1 tsp cinnamon
- 2 oz. almonds
- 2 oz. sunflower seeds

DIRECTIONS

1. **Place all ingredients, except orange juice, in a blender and blend until smooth**
2. **In a saucepan boil the orange juice and mix with the mixture and cook until the liquid has evaporated**
3. **Spread the mixture on a baking sheet**
4. **Bake at 350 F for 15-20 minutes**
5. **When ready remove from the oven cut into bars and serve**

FRENCH TOAST

Serves: ***4***

Prep Time: ***10*** Minutes

Cook Time: ***20*** Minutes

Total Time: ***30*** Minutes

INGREDIENTS

- **1 tablespoon olive oil**
- **4 eggs**
- **100 ml double cream**
- **¼ tsp cinnamon**
- **¼ tsp nutmeg**
- **¼ tsp peanut butter**
- **4 bread slices**

DIRECTIONS

1. **In a bowl combine all ingredients together and mix well**
2. **Place the bread into the dipping and let the bread soak for 3-4 minutes**
3. **In a skillet heat olive oil and fry the bread for 2-3 minutes per side**
4. **When ready remove from the skillet and serve**

BEANS OMELETTE

Serves: *1*

Prep Time: *5* Minutes

Cook Time: *10* Minutes

Total Time: *15* Minutes

INGREDIENTS

- 2 eggs
- ¼ tsp salt
- ¼ tsp black pepper
- 1 tablespoon olive oil
- ¼ cup cheese
- ¼ tsp basil
- 1 cup beans

DIRECTIONS

1. In a bowl combine all ingredients together and mix well
2. In a skillet heat olive oil and pour the egg mixture
3. Cook for 1-2 minutes per side
4. When ready remove omelette from the skillet and serve

BREAKFAST GRANOLA

Serves: 2
Prep Time: 5 Minutes

Cook Time: *30* Minutes

Total Time: *35* Minutes

INGREDIENTS

- 1 tsp vanilla extract
- 1 tablespoon honey
- 1 lb. rolled oats
- 2 tablespoons sesame seeds
- ¼ lb. almonds
- ¼ lb. berries

DIRECTIONS

1. Preheat the oven to 325 F
2. Spread the granola onto a baking sheet
3. Bake for 12-15 minutes, remove and mix everything
4. Bake for another 12-15 minutes or until slightly brown
5. When ready remove from the oven and serve

BLUEBERRY PANCAKES

Serves: *4*

Prep Time: *10* Minutes

Cook Time: *20* Minutes

Total Time: *30* Minutes

INGREDIENTS

- **1 cup whole wheat flour**
- **¼ tsp baking soda**
- **¼ tsp baking powder**
- **1 cup blueberries**
- **1 cup milk**

DIRECTIONS

1. **In a bowl combine all ingredients together and mix well**
2. **In a skillet heat olive oil**
3. **Pour ¼ of the batter and cook each pancake for 1-2 minutes per side**
4. **When ready remove from heat and serve**

CURRANTS PANCAKES

Serves: ***4***

Prep Time: ***10*** Minutes

Cook Time: ***30*** Minutes

Total Time: ***40*** Minutes

INGREDIENTS

- **1 cup whole wheat flour**
- **¼ tsp baking soda**
- **¼ tsp baking powder**
- **1 cup currants**
- **1 cup milk**

DIRECTIONS

1. **In a bowl combine all ingredients together and mix well**
2. **In a skillet heat olive oil**
3. **Pour ¼ of the batter and cook each pancake for 1-2 minutes per side**
4. **When ready remove from heat and serve**

COCONUT PANCAKES

Serves: *4*
Prep Time: *10* Minutes

Cook Time: *20* Minutes

Total Time: *30* Minutes

INGREDIENTS

- **1 cup whole wheat flour**
- **¼ tsp baking soda**
- **¼ tsp baking powder**
- **¼ cup coconut flakes**
- **1 cup milk**

DIRECTIONS

1. **In a bowl combine all ingredients together and mix well**
2. **In a skillet heat olive oil**
3. **Pour ¼ of the batter and cook each pancake for 1-2 minutes per side**
4. **When ready remove from heat and serve**

WALNUT PANCAKES

Serves: ***4***

Prep Time: ***10*** Minutes

Cook Time: ***20*** Minutes

Total Time: ***30*** Minutes

INGREDIENTS

- **1 cup whole wheat flour**
- **¼ tsp baking soda**
- **¼ tsp baking powder**
- **1 cup coconut flakes**
- **1 cup milk**

DIRECTIONS

1. **In a bowl combine all ingredients together and mix well**
2. **In a skillet heat olive oil**
3. **Pour ¼ of the batter and cook each pancake for 1-2 minutes per side**
4. **When ready remove from heat and serve**

PANCAKES

Serves: ***4***

Prep Time: ***10*** Minutes

Cook Time: ***30*** Minutes

Total Time: ***40*** Minutes

INGREDIENTS

- **1 cup whole wheat flour**
- **¼ tsp baking soda**
- **¼ tsp baking powder**
- **1 cup milk**

DIRECTIONS

1. **In a bowl combine all ingredients together and mix well**
2. **In a skillet heat olive oil**
3. **Pour ¼ of the batter and cook each pancake for 1-2 minutes per side**
4. **When ready remove from heat and serve**

RAISIN BREAKFAST MIX

Serves: *1*
Prep Time: *5* Minutes
Cook Time: *5* Minutes
Total Time: *10* Minutes

INGREDIENTS

- **½ cup dried raisins**
- **½ cup dried pecans**
- **¼ cup almonds**
- **1 cup coconut milk**
- **1 tsp cinnamon**

DIRECTIONS

1. **In a bowl combine all ingredients together**
2. **Serve with milk**

SAUSAGE BREAKFAST SANDWICH

Serves: 2

Prep Time: *5* Minutes

Cook Time: *15* Minutes

Total Time: *20* Minutes

INGREDIENTS

- ¼ cup egg substitute
- 1 muffin
- 1 turkey sausage patty
- 1 tablespoon cheddar cheese

DIRECTIONS

1. In a skillet pour egg and cook on low heat
2. Place turkey sausage patty in a pan and cook for 4-5 minutes per side
3. On a toasted muffin place the cooked egg, top with a sausage patty and cheddar cheese
4. Serve when ready

STRAWBERRY MUFFINS

Serves: *8-12*

Prep Time: ***10*** Minutes

Cook Time: ***20*** Minutes

Total Time: ***30*** Minutes

INGREDIENTS

- 2 eggs
- 1 tablespoon olive oil
- 1 cup milk
- 2 cups whole wheat flour
- 1 tsp baking soda
- ¼ tsp baking soda
- 1 tsp cinnamon
- 1 cup strawberries

DIRECTIONS

1. In a bowl combine all wet ingredients
2. In another bowl combine all dry ingredients
3. Combine wet and dry ingredients together
4. Pour mixture into 8-12 prepared muffin cups, fill 2/3 of the cups
5. Bake for 18-20 minutes at 375 F
6. When ready remove from the oven and serve

DESSERTS

BREAKFAST COOKIES

Serves: *8-12*
Prep Time: *5* Minutes

Cook Time: *15* Minutes

Total Time: *20* Minutes

INGREDIENTS

- **1 cup rolled oats**
- **¼ cup applesauce**
- **½ tsp vanilla extract**
- **3 tablespoons chocolate chips**
- **2 tablespoons dried fruits**
- **1 tsp cinnamon**

DIRECTIONS

1. **Preheat the oven to 325 F**
2. **In a bowl combine all ingredients together and mix well**
3. **Scoop cookies using an ice cream scoop**
4. **Place cookies onto a prepared baking sheet**
5. **Place in the oven for 12-15 minutes or until the cookies are done**
6. **When ready remove from the oven and serve**

BLUEBERRY PIE

Serves: *8-12*

Prep Time: *15* Minutes

Cook Time: *35* Minutes

Total Time: *50* Minutes

INGREDIENTS

- pastry sheets
- ¼ tsp lavender
- 1 cup brown sugar
- 4-5 cups blueberries
- 1 tablespoon lemon juice
- 1 cup almonds
- 2 tablespoons butter

DIRECTIONS

1. Line a pie plate or pie form with pastry and cover the edges of the plate depending on your preference
2. In a bowl combine all pie ingredients together and mix well
3. Pour the mixture over the pastry
4. Bake at 400-425 F for 25-30 minutes or until golden brown
5. When ready remove from the oven and let it rest for 15 minutes

PUMPKIN PIE

Serves: *8-12*

Prep Time: *15* Minutes

Cook Time: *35* Minutes

Total Time: *50* Minutes

INGREDIENTS

- pastry sheets
- 1 cup buttermilk
- 1 can pumpkin
- 1 cup sugar
- 1 tsp cinnamon
- 1 tsp vanilla extract
- 2 eggs

DIRECTIONS

1. Line a pie plate or pie form with pastry and cover the edges of the plate depending on your preference
2. In a bowl combine all pie ingredients together and mix well
3. Pour the mixture over the pastry
4. Bake at 400-425 F for 25-30 minutes or until golden brown
5. When ready remove from the oven and let it rest for 15 minutes

RICOTTA ICE-CREAM

Serves: *6-8*

Prep Time: *15* Minutes

Cook Time: *15* Minutes

Total Time: *30* Minutes

INGREDIENTS

- 1 cup almonds
- 1-pint vanilla ice cream
- 2 cups ricotta cheese
- 1 cup honey

DIRECTIONS

1. In a saucepan whisk together all ingredients
2. Mix until bubbly
3. Strain into a bowl and cool
4. Whisk in favorite fruits and mix well
5. Cover and refrigerate for 2-3 hours
6. Pour mixture in the ice-cream maker and follow manufacturer instructions
7. Serve when ready

SAFFRON ICE-CREAM

Serves: *6-8*

Prep Time: *15* Minutes

Cook Time: *15* Minutes

Total Time: *30* Minutes

INGREDIENTS

- **4 egg yolks**
- **1 cup heavy cream**
- **1 cup milk**
- **½ cup brown sugar**
- **1 tsp saffron**
- **1 tsp vanilla extract**

DIRECTIONS

1. **In a saucepan whisk together all ingredients**
2. **Mix until bubbly**
3. **Strain into a bowl and cool**
4. **Whisk in favorite fruits and mix well**
5. **Cover and refrigerate for 2-3 hours**
6. **Pour mixture in the ice-cream maker and follow manufacturer instructions**
7. **Serve when ready**

SMOOTHIES AND DRINKS

FIG SMOOTHIE

Serves: *1*

Prep Time: *5* Minutes

Cook Time: *5* Minutes

Total Time: *10* Minutes

INGREDIENTS

- **1 cup ice**
- **1 cup vanilla yogurt**
- **1 cup coconut milk**
- **1 tsp honey**
- **4 figs**

DIRECTIONS

1. **In a blender place all ingredients and blend until smooth**
2. **Pour smoothie in a glass and serve**

POMEGRANATE SMOOTHIE

Serves: *1*

Prep Time: *5* Minutes

Cook Time: *5* Minutes

Total Time: ***10*** Minutes

INGREDIENTS

- **2 cups blueberries**
- **1 cup pomegranate**
- **1 tablespoon honey**
- **1 cup Greek yogurt**

DIRECTIONS

1. **In a blender place all ingredients and blend until smooth**
2. **Pour smoothie in a glass and serve**

GINGER-KALE SMOOTHIE

Serves: *1*

Prep Time: *5* Minutes

Cook Time: *5* Minutes

Total Time: ***10*** Minutes

INGREDIENTS

- **1 cup kale**
- **1 banana**
- **1 cup almond milk**
- **1 cup vanilla yogurt**
- **1 tsp chia seeds**
- **¼ tsp ginger**

DIRECTIONS

1. **In a blender place all ingredients and blend until smooth**
2. **Pour smoothie in a glass and serve**

BERRY YOGHURT SMOOTHIE

Serves: *1*

Prep Time: *5* Minutes

Cook Time: *5* Minutes

Total Time: ***10*** Minutes

INGREDIENTS

- 6 oz. berries
- 2 bananas
- 4 oz. vanilla yoghurt
- 1 cup milk
- 1 tablespoon honey

DIRECTIONS

1. **In a blender place all ingredients and blend until smooth**
2. **Pour smoothie in a glass and serve**

COCONUT SMOOTHIE

Serves: *1*

Prep Time: *5* Minutes

Cook Time: *5* Minutes

Total Time: ***10*** Minutes

INGREDIENTS

- 2 mangoes
- 2 bananas
- 1 cup coconut water
- 1 cup ice
- 1 tablespoon honey
- 1 cup Greek Yoghurt
- 1 cup strawberries

DIRECTIONS

1. **In a blender place all ingredients and blend until smooth**
2. **Pour smoothie in a glass and serve**

RASPBERRY-VANILLA SMOOTHIE

Serves: *1*
Prep Time: *5* Minutes

Cook Time: *5* Minutes

Total Time: ***10*** Minutes

INGREDIENTS

- **¼ cup sugar**
- **¼ cup water**
- **1 cup Greek yoghurt**
- **1 cup raspberries**
- **1 tsp vanilla extract**
- **1 cup ice**

DIRECTIONS

1. **In a blender place all ingredients and blend until smooth**
2. **Pour smoothie in a glass and serve**

CHERRY SMOOTHIE

Serves: *1*
Prep Time: *5* Minutes

Cook Time: *5* Minutes

Total Time: ***10*** Minutes

INGREDIENTS

- **1 can cherries**
- **2 tablespoons peanut butter**
- **1 tablespoon honey**
- **1 cup Greek Yoghurt**
- **1 cup coconut milk**

DIRECTIONS

1. **In a blender place all ingredients and blend until smooth**
2. **Pour smoothie in a glass and serve**

CHOCOLATE SMOOTHIE

Serves: *1*

Prep Time: *5* Minutes

Cook Time: *5* Minutes

Total Time: *10* Minutes

INGREDIENTS

- 2 bananas
- 1 cup Greek Yoghurt
- 1 tablespoon honey
- 1 tablespoon cocoa powder
- ½ cup chocolate chips
- ¼ cup almond milk

DIRECTIONS

1. **In a blender place all ingredients and blend until smooth**
2. **Pour smoothie in a glass and serve**

TOFU SMOOTHIE

Serves: *1*

Prep Time: *5* Minutes

Cook Time: *5* Minutes

Total Time: ***10*** Minutes

INGREDIENTS

- **1 cup blueberries**
- **¼ cup tofu**
- **¼ cup pomegranate juice**
- **1 cup ice**
- **½ cup agave nectar**

DIRECTIONS

1. **In a blender place all ingredients and blend until smooth**
2. **Pour smoothie in a glass and serve**

ORANGE SMOOTHIE

Serves: *1*
Prep Time: *5* Minutes

Cook Time: *5* Minutes

Total Time: *10* Minutes

INGREDIENTS

- **1 orange**
- **½ cup orange juice**
- **½ banana**
- **1 tsp vanilla essence**

DIRECTIONS

1. **In a blender place all ingredients and blend until smooth**
2. **Pour smoothie in a glass and serve**

RAISIN DATE SMOOTHIE

Serves: *1*
Prep Time: *5* Minutes

Cook Time: *5* Minutes

Total Time: ***10*** Minutes

INGREDIENTS

- **¼ cup raisins**
- **2 Medjool dates**
- **1 cup berries**
- **1 cup almond milk**
- **1 tsp chia seeds**

DIRECTIONS

1. **In a blender place all ingredients and blend until smooth**
2. **Pour smoothie in a glass and serve**

FIFTH COOKBOOK

ZUCCHINI SOUP

Serves: ***4***

Prep Time: ***10*** Minutes

Cook Time: ***20*** Minutes

Total Time: ***30*** Minutes

INGREDIENTS

- **1 tablespoon olive oil**
- **1 lb. zucchini**
- **¼ red onion**
- **½ cup all-purpose flour**
- **¼ tsp salt**
- **¼ tsp pepper**
- **1 can vegetable broth**
- **1 cup heavy cream**

DIRECTIONS

1. **In a saucepan heat olive oil and sauté zucchini until tender**
2. **Add remaining ingredients to the saucepan and bring to a boil**
3. **When all the vegetables are tender transfer to a blender and blend until smooth**
4. **Pour soup into bowls, garnish with parsley and serve**

BROCCOLI SOUP

Serves: 2

Prep Time: *10* Minutes

Cook Time: *10* Minutes

Total Time: *20* Minutes

INGREDIENTS

- **1 onion**
- **2 cloves garlic**
- **1 tbs butter**
- **2 cup broccoli**
- **1 potato**
- **3 cup chicken broth**
- **1 cup cheddar cheese**
- **1/3 cup buttermilk**
- **Salt**
- **Pepper**

DIRECTIONS

1. **Cook the onion and garlic in melted butter for 5 minutes**
2. **Add the diced potato, broccoli florets and chicken broth**
3. **Bring to a boil, then reduce the heat and simmer for at least 5 minutes**
4. **Allow to cool, then pulse until smooth using a blender**

5. **Return to the saucepan and add the buttermilk and ¼ cup cheese**
6. **Cook for about 3 minutes**
7. **Season with salt and pepper**
8. **Serve topped with the remaining cheese**

CHICKEN NOODLE SOUP

Serves: ***6***

Prep Time: ***40*** Minutes

Cook Time: ***80*** Minutes

Total Time: ***120*** Minutes

INGREDIENTS

Broth:

- **15 peppercorns**
- **2 onions**
- **2 carrots**
- **1 rib celery**
- **3 sprigs thyme**
- **5 cloves garlic**
- **3 bay leaves**
- **8 chicken thighs**

Soup:

- **2 chicken bouillon cubes**
- **1 tsp salt**
- **5 oz egg noodles**
- **1/3 cup parsley**
- **2 ribs celery**
- **2 carrots**

DIRECTIONS

1. Place the broth ingredients in a pot with 12 cups of water
2. Bring to a boil, then reduce the heat and simmer for about 20 minutes
3. Remove the chicken and shred meat from bones
4. Return the bones to the pot and continue to simmer for another 60 minutes
5. Strain the broth and discard the bones and other solids
6. Skim broth and bring to a boil
7. Add the soup ingredients except for the parsley
8. Stir in the noodles and cook for at least 5 minutes
9. Stir in the chicken meat and parsley and cook 1 more minute
10. Serve immediately

TORTILLA SOUP

Serves: *6*

Prep Time: *10* Minutes

Cook Time: *10* Minutes

Total Time: *20* Minutes

INGREDIENTS

- 1/3 cup rice
- 15 oz salsa
- 1 can black beans
- 30 oz chicken broth
- 1 cup corn
- Chicken

DIRECTIONS

1. Place the broth and the salsa in a pot and bring to a boil
2. Add rice, beans and cooked chicken
3. Simmer covered for about 10 minutes
4. Stir in the corn
5. Serve topped with cheese

ASPARAGUS SOUP

Serves: *4*

Prep Time: *15* Minutes

Cook Time: *35* Minutes

Total Time: *50* Minutes

INGREDIENTS

- 2 tbs oil
- 1/3 tsp salt
- 1 cup bread cubes
- 1 cup potato
- 2 tsp horseradish
- 3 cups chicken broth
- 1 lb asparagus
- Scallions
- 1 shallot

DIRECTIONS

1. **Cook the shallot until soft for 2 minutes**
2. **Add the asparagus, potato, broth, horseradish and salt and bring to a boil**
3. **Reduce the heat and simmer for about 15 minutes**
4. **Pulse using a blender**
5. **Cook the bread cubes in hot oil until crispy, serve with croutons**

LENTIL SOUP

Serves: *9*

Prep Time: ***10*** Minutes

Cook Time: ***50*** Minutes

Total Time: ***60*** Minutes

INGREDIENTS

- **2 tbs oil**
- **1 stalk celery**
- **1 red bell pepper**
- **2 cans chicken broth**
- **1 onion**
- **1 cup carrots**
- **2 garlic cloves**
- **2 tsp cumin**
- **1 tsp coriander**
- **1 can tomatoes**
- **2 sweet potatoes**
- **3 tsp thyme leaves**
- **2 cups red lentils**

DIRECTIONS

1. **Cook the onion, celery, carrots and red pepper in hot oil for 3 minutes**

2. Add garlic, thyme, cumin and coriander and cook for 10 more minutes
3. Add the broth, sweet potatoes, lentils and tomatoes
4. Bring to a boil, then reduce the heat and simmer for at least 30 minutes
5. Pulse using a blender
6. Serve immediately

BROCCOLI AND RED CAPSICUM SOUP

Serves: *4*

Prep Time: *10* Minutes

Cook Time: *15* Minutes

Total Time: *25* Minutes

INGREDIENTS

- 1 cup broccoli florets
- 1 cup red capsicum
- 1 tsp oil
- 1 tablespoon garlic
- ¼ cup onions
- pinch of salt
- 1 tsp pepper powder

DIRECTIONS

1. In a pan sauté onions and garlic for 2-3 minutes
2. Add salt, red capsicum, broccoli, 1 cup water, and mix well
3. Cover with a lid cook for 5-6 minutes
4. When ready remove from heat and blend using a mixer
5. Transfer the mixture back to the pan, add ¼ cup water, pepper powder and cook for another 2-3 minutes
6. When ready remove from heat and serve

CANTALOUPE SOUP

Serves: *4*

Prep Time: *10* Minutes

Cook Time: *15* Minutes

Total Time: *25* Minutes

INGREDIENTS

- 2 cantaloupes
- 1 tsp ginger
- ½ tsp nutmeg
- ½ cup fat-free sour cream

DIRECTIONS

1. **Remove seeds from cantaloupes and refrigerate**
2. **Pour melon into a blender with spices, sour cream and blend until smooth**
3. **Refrigerate for another hour and pour soup into the bowl**
4. **Garnish with nutmeg, ginger and serve**

GREEN PESTO PASTA

Serves: 2

Prep Time: *5* Minutes

Cook Time: *15* Minutes

Total Time: *20* Minutes

INGREDIENTS

- 4 oz. spaghetti
- 2 cups basil leaves
- 2 garlic cloves
- ¼ cup olive oil
- 2 tablespoons parmesan cheese
- ½ tsp black pepper

DIRECTIONS

1. Bring water to a boil and add pasta
2. In a blend add parmesan cheese, basil leaves, garlic and blend
3. Add olive oil, pepper and blend again
4. Pour pesto onto pasta and serve when ready

BUCKWHEAT DOSA

Serves: *4*

Prep Time: *5* Minutes

Cook Time: *20* Minutes

Total Time: *25* Minutes

INGREDIENTS

- **1 cup buckwheat**
- **1 tablespoon olive oil**
- **1 tsp mustard seeds**
- **½ tsp asafetida**
- **1 tsp green chilies**
- **1 tablespoon coriander**
- **1 tablespoon urad dal**

DIRECTIONS

1. **In a bowl combine urad dal and buckwheat, using a mixer blend until smooth**
2. **In a pan add mustard seeds, asafetida, chilies, salt, coriander, water, and mix well**
3. **Pour 1/3 cup batter in a circular manner and cook until golden brown**
4. **When ready remove and serve**

ZUCCHINI BAJRA KHICHDI

Serves: *3*

Prep Time: *10* Minutes

Cook Time: *30* Minutes

Total Time: *40* Minutes

INGREDIENTS

- ½ cup zucchini
- ¼ cup bajra
- 1 tsp olive oil
- 1 tsp cumin seeds
- ¼ cup red capsicum
- ¼ cup green capsicum
- ¼ cup almond milk
- ¼ tsp chili paste
- ¼ cup coriander

DIRECTIONS

1. Soak the bajra in water overnight
2. In a pressure cooker combine water, bajra and mix well
3. Allow the steam to go away before opening the lid
4. In a pan add cumin seeds, asafetida and sauté for 1-2 minutes
5. Add capsicum, zucchini, salt and sauté for another 3-4 minutes

6. **Add milk, coriander, chili paste and cook for another 2-3 minutes**
7. **When ready remove from heat and serve**

QUINOA MUTHIA

Serves: *5*

Prep Time: *10* Minutes

Cook Time: *40* Minutes

Total Time: *50* Minutes

INGREDIENTS

- ½ cup quinoa flour
- 1 cup besan
- ¼ cup semolina
- 1 cup bottle gourd
- 6 tsp oil
- 2 tsp chilli paste
- 1 pinch baking soda
- ¼ tsp asafetida
- ¼ tsp turmeric powder
- 1 tsp lemon juice
- 1 tsp mustard seeds
- 1 tsp sesame seeds
- 3 curry leaves
- 1 tablespoon coriander

DIRECTIONS

1. In a bowl combine semolina, besan, quinoa flour, 1 tsp oil, chili paste, gourd, asafetida, turmeric powder, lemon juice, and salt
2. Divide mixture into 4-5 portions and shape them into patties
3. Steam in a steamer for 10-15 minutes
4. When ready, remove from the steamer
5. In a pan add remaining oil, sesame seeds, curry leaves, asafetida and sauté for 1 minute
6. Add muthia, sauté for 2-3 minutes and serve with coriander

LIME GRILLED CORN

Serves: *3*

Prep Time: *5* Minutes

Cook Time: *15* Minutes

Total Time: *20* Minutes

INGREDIENTS

- **3 ears of corn**
- **2 tablespoons mayonnaise**
- **2 tablespoons squeezed lime juice**
- **½ tsp chili powder**
- **1 pinch of salt**

DIRECTIONS

1. **Place corn onto the grill and cook for 5-6 minutes or until the kernels being to brown**
2. **Turn every few minutes until all sides are slightly charred**
3. **In a bowl mix the rest of ingredients**
4. **Spread a light coating of the mixture onto each corn and serve**

CAPSICUM AND PANEER SUBZI

Serves: *5*

Prep Time: *10* Minutes

Cook Time: *15* Minutes

Total Time: *25* Minutes

INGREDIENTS

- **2 cups capsicum cubes**
- **¼ cup paneer**
- **1 tsp oil**
- **¼ cup onion cubes**
- **¼ tsp ginger paste**
- **1 tsp garlic paste**
- **1 tsp dried fenugreek leaves**
- **1 cup tomato pulp**
- **¼ tsp turmeric powder**
- **¼ tsp chili powder**
- **1 tsp garam masala**
- **pinch of salt**

DIRECTIONS

1. **In a pan sauté onion**
2. **Add garlic paste, fenugreek leaves, ginger paste and sauté for 1 minute**

3. Add capsicum, turmeric powder, tomato pulp, chili powder, garam masala and mix well
4. Cook for 5-6 minutes, add salt, paneer and mix well
5. Cook for another 2-3 minutes, when ready remove from heat and serve

AVOCADO DIP

Serves: ***4***

Prep Time: *5* Minutes

Cook Time: *5* Minutes

Total Time: ***10*** Minutes

INGREDIENTS

- **1 cup mashed avocado**
- **1 tsp lemon juice**
- **1 tablespoon tomatoes**
- **¼ tsp green chilies**
- **pinch of salt**

DIRECTIONS

1. **In a bowl combine all ingredients together and mix well**
2. **When ready serve with corn chips**

ONION PURIS

Serves: *28*

Prep Time: *5* Minutes

Cook Time: *20* Minutes

Total Time: *25* Minutes

INGREDIENTS

- ½ cup jowar
- ½ cup onions
- 1 tsp sesame seeds
- pinch of salt
- ¼ tsp oil

DIRECTIONS

1. In a bowl combine all ingredients together
2. Divide dough into 22-28 portions
3. Press each portion of dough between your hands until it looks like a thin circle
4. Grease a baking tray with oil
5. Bake for 18-20 minutes at 350 F
6. When ready remove and serve

KALE CHIPS

Serves: *6*

Prep Time: *10* Minutes

Cook Time: *25* Minutes

Total Time: *35* Minutes

INGREDIENTS

- 1 bunch of kale
- 1 tablespoon olive oil
- 1 tsp salt

DIRECTIONS

1. Preheat the oven to 325 F
2. Chop the kale into chip size pieces
3. Put pieces into a bowl tops with olive oil and salt
4. Spread the leaves in a single layer onto a parchment paper
5. Bake for 20-25 minutes
6. When ready, remove and serve

CRANBERRY SALAD

Serves: 2

Prep Time: *5* Minutes

Cook Time: *5* Minutes

Total Time: ***10*** Minutes

INGREDIENTS

- **1 can unsweetened pineapple**
- **1 package cherry gelatin**
- **1 tablespoon lemon juice**
- **½ cup artificial sweetener**
- **1 cup cranberries**
- **1 orange**
- **1 cup celery**
- **½ cup pecans**

DIRECTIONS

1. **In a bowl mix all ingredients and mix well**
2. **Serve with dressing**

ITALIAN SALAD

Serves: 2

Prep Time: *5* Minutes

Cook Time: *5* Minutes

Total Time: ***10*** Minutes

INGREDIENTS

- **8 oz. romaine lettuce**
- **2 cups radicchio**
- **¼ red onion**
- **2 ribs celery**
- **1 cup tomatoes**
- **1 can chickpeas**
- **1 cup salad dressing**

DIRECTIONS

1. **In a bowl mix all ingredients and mix well**
2. **Serve with dressing**

CHICKPEA COLESLAW

Serves: 2

Prep Time: 5 Minutes

Cook Time: 5 Minutes

Total Time: *10* Minutes

INGREDIENTS

- **2 cans chickpeas**
- **2 cups carrots**
- **1 cup celery**
- **¼ cup green onions**
- **¼ cup dill leaves**
- **¼ cup olive oil**
- **1 cucumber**
- **1 cup salad dressing**

DIRECTIONS

1. In a bowl mix all ingredients and mix well

2. Serve with dressing

ROMAINE SALAD

Serves: 2

Prep Time: *5* Minutes

Cook Time: *5* Minutes

Total Time: ***10*** Minutes

INGREDIENTS

- **1 cup cooked quinoa**
- **1 cup sunflower seeds**
- **1 tablespoon olive oil**
- **1 head romaine lettuce**
- **1 cup carrots**
- **1 cup cabbage**
- **¼ cup radishes**

DIRECTIONS

1. **In a bowl mix all ingredients and mix well**
2. **Serve with dressing**

GRAIN SALAD

Serves: 2

Prep Time: *5* Minutes

Cook Time: *5* Minutes

Total Time: ***10*** Minutes

INGREDIENTS

- **1 bunch coriander leaves**
- **1 bunch mint leaves**
- **¼ red onion**
- **1 bunch parsley**
- **1 cup lentils**
- **1 tablespoon pumpkin seeds**
- **1 tablespoon pine nuts**

DIRECTIONS

1. **In a bowl mix all ingredients and mix well**
2. **Serve with dressing**

QUINOA SALAD

Serves: 2
Prep Time: 5 Minutes

Cook Time: 5 Minutes

Total Time: *10* Minutes

INGREDIENTS

- **1 cauliflower**
- **2 cups cooked quinoa**
- **1 can chickpeas**
- **1 cup baby spinach**
- **¼ cup parsley**
- **¼ cup cilantro**
- **¼ cup green onion**
- **½ cup feta cheese**

DIRECTIONS

1. **In a bowl mix all ingredients and mix well**
2. **Serve with dressing**

WEDGE SALAD

Serves: 2

Prep Time: *5* Minutes

Cook Time: *5* Minutes

Total Time: ***10*** Minutes

INGREDIENTS

- **1 head romaine lettuce**
- **1 cup tomatoes**
- **1 cup cucumber**
- **1 cup celery**
- **¼ cup olives**
- **1 shallot**
- **1 cup salad dressing**

DIRECTIONS

1. **In a bowl mix all ingredients and mix well**
2. **Serve with dressing**

COUSCOUS SALAD

Serves: 2
Prep Time: 5 Minutes

Cook Time: 5 Minutes

Total Time: ***10*** Minutes

INGREDIENTS

- **1 cup couscous**
- **¼ cup pine nuts**
- **¼ cup olive lil**
- **1 tablespoon lemon juice**
- **1 shallot**
- **2 cloves garlic**
- **1 tsp salt**
- **1 can chickpeas**
- **1 cup tomatoes**
- **½ cup feta cheese**
- **1 zucchini**
- **1 tablespoon basil**

DIRECTIONS

1. **In a bowl mix all ingredients and mix well**
2. **Serve with dressing**

FARRO SALAD

Serves: 2

Prep Time: 5 Minutes

Cook Time: 5 Minutes

Total Time: *10* Minutes

INGREDIENTS

- **1 cup cooked FARRO**
- **1 bay leaf**
- **1 shallot**
- **¼ cup olive oil**
- **2 cups arugula**
- **¼ cup parmesan cheese**
- **¼ cup basil**
- **¼ cup parsley**
- **¼ cup pecans**

DIRECTIONS

1. **In a bowl mix all ingredients and mix well**
2. **Serve with dressing**

THAI MANGO SALAD

Serves: 2
Prep Time: *5* Minutes

Cook Time: *5* Minutes

Total Time: ***10*** Minutes

INGREDIENTS

- **1 head leaf lettuce**
- **1 red bell pepper**
- **2 mangoes**
- **¼ green onion**
- **¼ cup peanuts**
- **¼ cup cilantro**
- **1 cup peanut dressing**

DIRECTIONS

1. **In a bowl mix all ingredients and mix well**
2. **Serve with dressing**

LENTIL FRITATTA

Serves: 2

Prep Time: *10* Minutes

Cook Time: *20* Minutes

Total Time: *30* Minutes

INGREDIENTS

- **½ lb. lentil**
- **1 tablespoon olive oil**
- **½ red onion**
- **¼ tsp salt**
- **2 eggs**
- **2 oz. cheddar cheese**
- **1 garlic clove**
- **¼ tsp dill**

DIRECTIONS

1. **In a bowl whisk eggs with salt and cheese**
2. **In a frying pan heat olive oil and pour egg mixture**
3. **Add remaining ingredients and mix well**
4. **Serve when ready**

SPINACH FRITATTA

Serves: 2

Prep Time: *10* Minutes

Cook Time: *20* Minutes

Total Time: *30* Minutes

INGREDIENTS

- ½ lb. spinach
- 1 tablespoon olive oil
- ½ red onion
- 2 eggs
- ¼ tsp salt
- 2 oz. cheddar cheese
- 1 garlic clove
- ¼ tsp dill

DIRECTIONS

1. In a skillet sauté spinach until tender
2. In a bowl whisk eggs with salt and cheese
3. In a frying pan heat olive oil and pour egg mixture
4. Add remaining ingredients and mix well
5. When ready serve with sautéed spinach

BLACK BEAN FRITATTA

Serves: **2**

Prep Time: ***10*** Minutes

Cook Time: ***20*** Minutes

Total Time: ***30*** Minutes

INGREDIENTS

- **1 cup cooked black beans**
- **1 tablespoon olive oil**
- **½ red onion**
- **¼ tsp salt**
- **2 oz. cheddar cheese**
- **1 garlic clove**
- **¼ tsp dill**
- **2 eggs**

DIRECTIONS

1. **In a bowl whisk eggs with salt and cheese**
2. **In a frying pan heat olive oil and pour egg mixture**
3. **Add remaining ingredients and mix well**
4. **Serve when ready**

CHEESE FRITATTA

Serves: *2*

Prep Time: *10* Minutes

Cook Time: *20* Minutes

Total Time: *30* Minutes

INGREDIENTS

- 1 tablespoon olive oil
- ½ red onion
- ¼ tsp salt
- 2 oz. cheddar cheese
- 1 garlic clove
- ¼ tsp dill
- 2 eggs

DIRECTIONS

1. In a bowl combine cheddar cheese and onion
2. In a frying pan heat olive oil and pour egg mixture
3. Add remaining ingredients and mix well
4. Serve when ready

BROCCOLI FRITATTA

Serves: 2

Prep Time: *10* Minutes

Cook Time: *20* Minutes

Total Time: *30* Minutes

INGREDIENTS

- 1 cup broccoli
- 1 tablespoon olive oil
- ½ red onion
- ¼ tsp salt
- 2 oz. cheddar cheese
- 1 garlic clove
- 2 eggs
- ¼ tsp dill

DIRECTIONS

1. In a skillet sauté broccoli until tender
2. In a bowl whisk eggs with salt and cheese
3. In a frying pan heat olive oil and pour egg mixture
4. Add remaining ingredients and mix well
5. When ready serve with sautéed broccoli

SHAKSHUKA

Serves: ***2***

Prep Time: ***10*** Minutes

Cook Time: ***20*** Minutes

Total Time: ***30*** Minutes

INGREDIENTS

- **1 tablespoon olive oil**
- **1 red onion**
- **1 red chili**
- **1 garlic clove**
- **2 cans cherry tomatoes**
- **2 eggs**

DIRECTIONS

1. **In a frying pan cook garlic, chili, onions until soft**
2. **Stir in tomatoes and cook until mixture thickens**
3. **Crack the eggs over the sauce**
4. **Cover with a lid and cook for another 7-8 minutes**
5. **When ready remove from heat and serve**

BROCCOLI CASSEROLE

Serves: *4*

Prep Time: *10* Minutes

Cook Time: *15* Minutes

Total Time: *25* Minutes

INGREDIENTS

- 1 onion
- 2 chicken breasts
- 2 tablespoons unsalted butter
- 2 eggs
- 2 cups cooked rice
- 2 cups cheese
- 1 cup parmesan cheese
- 2 cups cooked broccoli

DIRECTIONS

1. Sauté the veggies and set aside
2. Preheat the oven to 425 F
3. Transfer the sautéed veggies to a baking dish, add remaining ingredients to the baking dish
4. Mix well, add seasoning and place the dish in the oven
5. Bake for 12-15 minutes or until slightly brown
6. When ready remove from the oven and serve

BEAN FRITATTA

Serves: *2*

Prep Time: *10* Minutes

Cook Time: *20* Minutes

Total Time: *30* Minutes

INGREDIENTS

- 1 cup black beans
- 1 tablespoon olive oil
- ½ red onion
- 2 eggs
- ¼ tsp salt
- 2 oz. cheddar cheese
- 1 garlic clove
- ¼ tsp dill

DIRECTIONS

1. In a bowl whisk eggs with salt and cheese
2. In a frying pan heat olive oil and pour egg mixture
3. Add remaining ingredients and mix well
4. Serve when ready

ROASTED SQUASH

Serves: *3-4*

Prep Time: *10* Minutes

Cook Time: *20* Minutes

Total Time: *30* Minutes

INGREDIENTS

- 2 delicata squashes
- 2 tablespoons olive oil
- 1 tsp curry powder
- 1 tsp salt

DIRECTIONS

1. **Preheat the oven to 400 F**
2. **Cut everything in half lengthwise**
3. **Toss everything with olive oil and place onto a prepared baking sheet**
4. **Roast for 18-20 minutes at 400 F or until golden brown**
5. **When ready remove from the oven and serve**

POTATO CHIPS

Serves: *2*

Prep Time: *10* Minutes

Cook Time: *20* Minutes

Total Time: *30* Minutes

INGREDIENTS

- 1 lb. sweet. potatoes
- 2 tablespoons olive oil
- 1 tablespoon smoked paprika
- 1 tablespoon salt

DIRECTIONS

1. Preheat the oven to 425 F
2. In a bowl toss everything with olive oil and seasoning
3. Spread everything onto a prepared baking sheet
4. Bake for 8-10 minutes or until crisp
5. When ready remove from the oven and serve

ZUCCHINI CHIPS

Serves: 2

Prep Time: *10* Minutes

Cook Time: *20* Minutes

Total Time: *30* Minutes

INGREDIENTS

- 1 lb. zucchini
- 2 tablespoons olive oil
- 1 tablespoon smoked paprika
- 1 tablespoon salt

DIRECTIONS

1. Preheat the oven to 425 F
2. In a bowl toss everything with olive oil and seasoning
3. Spread everything onto a prepared baking sheet
4. Bake for 8-10 minutes or until crisp
5. When ready remove from the oven and serve

ZUCCHINI PIZZA CRUST

Serves: ***4***

Prep Time: ***10*** Minutes

Cook Time: ***30*** Minutes

Total Time: ***40*** Minutes

INGREDIENTS

- **4 zucchinis**
- **2 tsp salt**
- **2 cups almond flour**
- **2 tablespoons coconut flour**
- **3 eggs**
- **2 ½ cups cheddar cheese**
- **1 tsp red pepper flakes**
- **1 tsp dried oregano**

DIRECTIONS

1. **Shred the zucchini, sprinkle with salt and set aside**
2. **Preheat the oven to 400 F**
3. **Mix zucchini with remaining ingredients**
4. **Place the dough over a baking sheet and spread evenly**

5. **Pop the pizza crust in the oven for 30 minutes or until golden brown**
6. **When ready, remove and serve**

BARBEQUE PIZZA

Serves: 2

Prep Time: *10* Minutes

Cook Time: *15* Minutes

Total Time: *25* Minutes

INGREDIENTS

- 1 pizza crust
- 1 tsp olive oil
- 1 cup onion
- ¼ cup red pepper strips
- 1 cup cooked chicken
- ¼ cup barbecue sauce
- 1 cup mozzarella cheese

DIRECTIONS

1. In a frying pan add pepper strips, onion and fry until soft
2. Add barbecue sauce, chicken and stir well
3. On a ready-made pizza crust spread onion, pepper mix, chicken and top with mozzarella
4. Bake for 12-15 minutes at 425 F

SHRIMP PIZZA

Serves: *4*

Prep Time: *5* Minutes

Cook Time: *20* Minutes

Total Time: *25* Minutes

INGREDIENTS

- 1 package pizza dough
- 1 tablespoon cornmeal
- 1/3 cup ricotta cheese
- 1 lb. shrimp
- 5 cloves roasted garlic
- 2 ¼ cups mozzarella cheese
- 1 tablespoon basil

DIRECTIONS

1. **Stretch pizza dough across a baking pan and bake for 6-8 minutes, sprinkle cornmeal over the pan**
2. **Mix ricotta cheese, garlic, shrimp together and place over pizza crust**
3. **Cover pizza with mozzarella and basil**
4. **Bake for 12-15 minutes at 425 F**

CAULIFLOWER CRUST PIZZA

Serves: *4*

Prep Time: *10* Minutes

Cook Time: *20* Minutes

Total Time: *30* Minutes

INGREDIENTS

- 1 lb. ground beef
- 1 egg
- 1 tsp parsley
- 1 tsp dried basil
- ¼ tsp salt
- ½ tsp pepper
- ¼ cup tomato puree
- 1 tsp tomato paste
- ¼ red pepper
- 1 tsp dried basil
- ¼ cup olives
- 5 slices prosciutto
- 4 oz. parmesan
- 1 handful fresh basil

DIRECTIONS

1. Preheat the oven to 430 F
2. In a bowl add salt, mince, egg, basil, pepper, parsley and mix well
3. Roll into a ball and place on a baking tray
4. Bake for 12-15 minutes
5. Mix the tomato paste with tomato puree and spread across the base
6. Top with peppers, prosciutto, parmesan, olives and bake for another 8-10 minutes
7. Remove from the oven, top with basil leaves and serve

SIXTH COOKBOOK

ROASTED ONION

Serves: ***3-4***

Prep Time: ***10*** Minutes

Cook Time: ***20*** Minutes

Total Time: ***30*** Minutes

INGREDIENTS

- 1 lb. onion
- 2 tablespoons olive oil
- 1 tsp curry powder
- 1 tsp salt

DIRECTIONS

1. Preheat the oven to 400 F
2. Cut everything in half lengthwise
3. Toss everything with olive oil and place onto a prepared baking sheet
4. Roast for 18-20 minutes at 400 F or until golden brown
5. When ready remove from the oven and serve

ROASTED SQUASH

Serves: *3-4*

Prep Time: *10* Minutes

Cook Time: *20* Minutes

Total Time: *30* Minutes

INGREDIENTS

- 2 delicata squashes
- 2 tablespoons olive oil
- 1 tsp curry powder
- 1 tsp salt

DIRECTIONS

1. **Preheat the oven to 400 F**
2. **Cut everything in half lengthwise**
3. **Toss everything with olive oil and place onto a prepared baking sheet**
4. **Roast for 18-20 minutes at 400 F or until golden brown**
5. **When ready remove from the oven and serve**

ROASTED GARLIC

Serves: 2

Prep Time: *10* Minutes

Cook Time: *10* Minutes

Total Time: *20* Minutes

INGREDIENTS

- **1 head garlic**
- **1 tablespoon olive oil**

DIRECTIONS

1. **Preheat oven to 375 F**
2. **Ove the garlic drizzle the olive oil and add to the pan**
3. **Roast for 15-20 minutes and remove from the oven**
4. **Let it cool and serve**

ZUCCHINI SOUP

Serves: ***4***

Prep Time: ***10*** Minutes

Cook Time: ***20*** Minutes

Total Time: ***30*** Minutes

INGREDIENTS

- **1 tablespoon olive oil**
- **1 lb. zucchini**
- **¼ red onion**
- **½ cup all-purpose flour**
- **¼ tsp salt**
- **¼ tsp pepper**
- **1 can vegetable broth**
- **1 cup heavy cream**

DIRECTIONS

1. **In a saucepan heat olive oil and sauté zucchini until tender**
2. **Add remaining ingredients to the saucepan and bring to a boil**
3. **When all the vegetables are tender transfer to a blender and blend until smooth**
4. **Pour soup into bowls, garnish with parsley and serve**

CREAMY CAULIFLOWER SOUP

Serves: *3*

Prep Time: ***10*** Minutes

Cook Time: ***50*** Minutes

Total Time: ***60*** Minutes

INGREDIENTS

- **1 head cauliflower**
- **1 apple**
- **1 tablespoon olive oil**
- **2 cups almond milk**
- **1 tablespoon fresh basil**
- **1 tsp curry powder**
- **1 tsp sesame seeds**

DIRECTIONS

1. **Preheat oven to 350 F and place the cauliflower on a prepared baking sheet**
2. **Drizzle with salt, pepper and olive oil**
3. **Roast for 40-45 minutes and remove from the oven**
4. **In a blender mix the cauliflower with the rest of the ingredients until smooth**
5. **Season with sesame seeds and serve**

SWEET POTATO SOUP

Serves: *3*

Prep Time: *10* Minutes

Cook Time: *50* Minutes

Total Time: *60* Minutes

INGREDIENTS

- 1 sweet potato
- 1 tsp olive oil
- 1 lbs. cranberries
- ½ cup water
- 1 tablespoon cashew butter
- 1 tsp salt

DIRECTIONS

1. **Preheat oven to 350 F and place the potatoes on a baking sheet, rub them with olive oil and roast for 45-50 minutes**
2. **Meanwhile cook the cranberries until tender, remove from the heat when ready**
3. **Remove the sweet potato from the oven and place blend it in a blender with cranberries and cashew butter and salt**
4. **Pour in a bowl and serve**

GREEN PESTO PASTA

Serves: 2

Prep Time: *5* Minutes

Cook Time: *15* Minutes

Total Time: *20* Minutes

INGREDIENTS

- 4 oz. spaghetti
- 2 cups basil leaves
- 2 garlic cloves
- ¼ cup olive oil
- 2 tablespoons parmesan cheese
- ½ tsp black pepper

DIRECTIONS

1. Bring water to a boil and add pasta
2. In a blend add parmesan cheese, basil leaves, garlic and blend
3. Add olive oil, pepper and blend again
4. Pour pesto onto pasta and serve when ready

FAJITA LETTUCE WRAPS

Serves: 2
Prep Time: *10* Minutes

Cook Time: *10* Minutes

Total Time: *20* Minutes

INGREDIENTS

- **2 tablespoons olive oil**
- **1 onion**
- **¼ cumin**
- **¼ cup tomatoes**
- **1 tablespoon walnuts**
- **2 tablespoons parsley**
- **3 carrots**
- **1 zucchini**
- **¼ tsp salt**
- **¼ tsp pepper**
- **¼ tsp cinnamon**

DIRECTIONS

1. **In a skillet sauté the olive oil and onion over low heat**
2. **Add carrots and zucchini and cook for 5-6 minutes**
3. **Add cinnamon, pepper and salt and cook for 1-2 minutes**

4. **Spoon into lettuce leaves and add walnuts, parsley and tomatoes**

FAJITAS WITH BASIL SAUCE

Serves: 2

Prep Time: *10* Minutes

Cook Time: *20* Minutes

Total Time: *30* Minutes

INGREDIENTS

- **½ cup quinoa**
- **1 cup water**
- **½ cup onion**
- **1 tablespoon parsley**
- **1 tsp lemon zest**
- **6 tortillas**
- **1 can cannellini beans**
- **1 pint cheery tomatoes**
- **1 cucumber**

Basil sauce

- **8 tomatillos**
- **2 tablespoons cannellini beans**
- **1 cucumber**
- **1 tablespoon almond butter**
- **3 basil leaves**

DIRECTIONS

1. **Hold tortilla over flame to low heat for 3-4 seconds each side**
2. **Cook quinoa for 10-15 minutes and remove form heat**
3. **Puree the basil sauce ingredients in a blender**
4. **Season with salt and pepper and serve**

BRUSEELS SPROUTS WITH BALSAMIC GLAZE

Serves: ***3***

Prep Time: ***10*** Minutes

Cook Time: ***40*** Minutes

Total Time: ***50*** Minutes

INGREDIENTS

- **1 head garlic**
- **1 lbs. Brussels sprouts**
- **1 tablespoon olive oil**
- **1 kale**
- **½ cup cabbage**
- **1 tablespoon almonds**
- **1 tsp lemon zest**
- **1 tablespoon cherries**

Balsamic Glaze

- **½ cup tahini**
- **1 tablespoon balsamic vinegar**
- **1 tablespoon lemon juice**
- **salt**
- **pepper**

DIRECTIONS

1. **Preheat oven to 375 F and place a baking sheet with parchment paper**
2. **Slice the garlic and drizzle it and Brussels sprouts with oil, salt and pepper**
3. **Place them on the baking sheet and roast for 25-30 minutes, remove them when ready**
4. **Drizzle with balsamic glaze (mix all the ingredients in a bowl)**

ROASTED SWEET POTATOES

Serves: *4*

Prep Time: *10* Minutes

Cook Time: *50* Minutes

Total Time: *60* Minutes

INGREDIENTS

- **2 sweet potatoes**
- **1 tsp olive oil**

Sauce

- **½ avocado diced**
- **¼ peach halves**
- **3 basil leaves**
- **1 tablespoon red onion**
- **2 tablespoons water**
- **¼ navel orange juiced**

DIRECTIONS

1. **Preheat the oven to 375 F and place the sweet potatoes on a baking sheet**
2. **Rub them with olive oil and roast for 40-45 minutes and remove from oven when ready**
3. **For sauce combine all the ingredients in a blender**

SPAGHETTI SQUASH PLATTER

Serves: *3*

Prep Time: *10* Minutes

Cook Time: *40* Minutes

Total Time: *50* Minutes

INGREDIENTS

- **1 spaghetti squash**
- **1 tablespoon onion**
- **1 avocado peeled**
- **1 whole pear**
- **1 tablespoon cashews**
- **1 tablespoon nuts**
- **1 tablespoon cherries**
- **1 tablespoon fresh dill**
- **1 tsp sesame seeds**
- **1 tablespoon olive oil**
- **1 cucumber**

Tahini Garlic Dressing

- **½ cup tahini**
- **1 clove garlic**
- **¼ cup water**

DIRECTIONS

1. Preheat oven to 350 F and place squash on a baking sheet and drizzle with olive oil and salt
2. Roast for 40-45 minutes and remove from oven when ready
3. Scoop out the spaghetti squash except the sesame seeds and dill
4. Mix all the ingredients in a bowl and drizzle over the squash and sprinkle with the dill

ROASTED CAULIFLOWER AND RICE PLATTER

Serves: *4*

Prep Time: *10* Minutes

Cook Time: *30* Minutes

Total Time: *40* Minutes

INGREDIENTS

- **1 large head cauliflower**
- **1 red pepper**
- **2 tablespoons red onion**
- **1 tablespoon macadamia nuts**
- **1 scallion**
- **1 fresh basil leave**
- **1 can sardines**
- **1 tablespoon olive oil**
- **½ cup wild rice**

DIRECTIONS

1. **Preheat oven to 375 F and line a baking sheet**
2. **Place the cauliflower on the baking sheet and drizzle with olive oil and salt**
3. **Roast for 20-25 minutes and remove when ready**
4. **Cook the rice and place it on a platter and add the cauliflower, season with salt and serve**

SALAD WITH KALE CAULIFLOWER

Serves: 2

Prep Time: *10* Minutes

Cook Time: *20* Minutes

Total Time: *30* Minutes

INGREDIENTS

- **1 head cauliflower**
- **1 cup arugula**
- **1 tablespoon sunflower seeds**
- **¼ cup tahini**
- **1 garlic clove**
- **1 tablespoon olive oil**
- **1 head purple kale**
- **1 cup cherry tomatoes**
- **1 head cabbage**
- **1 cup green grapes**

DIRECTIONS

1. **Preheat the oven to 375 F and place the cauliflower on a baking sheet and drizzle with olive oil and salt**
2. **Roast for 20-25 minutes and remove when ready**
3. **In a bowl combine cabbage, grapes, arugula, sunflower seeds, kale and tomatoes**

4. **In bowl mix tahini and garlic clove and drizzle over the salad**

GRAIN FREE FAJITAS

Serves: *3*

Prep Time: ***10*** Minutes

Cook Time: ***10*** Minutes

Total Time: ***20*** Minutes

INGREDIENTS

- **1 tablespoon avocado oil**
- **3 carrots**
- **3 large nori sheets**
- **1 tomato**
- **1 tablespoon fresh cilantro**
- **1 red pepper**
- **1 green bell pepper**
- **1 while onion**
- **1 jalapeno**

DIRECTIONS

1. **In a skillet sauce avocado oil, onion, jalapeno, white onion, salt and pepper for 6-7 minutes**
2. **Remove from heat and place mixture in a bowl**
3. **Sauté carrots with pepper and salt for 5-6 minutes**
4. **Combine coconut milk with curry powder and combine with red onion, sea s alt and pepper**

5. **Lay the nori sheets and top with pepper mixture and carrots and drizzle with coconut milk**

LIME SPINACH CHIPS

Serves: *6*

Prep Time: *10* Minutes

Cook Time: *30* Minutes

Total Time: *40* Minutes

INGREDIENTS

- **1 whole lime**
- **¼ tsp salt**
- **6 cups spinach**
- **2 tablespoons olive oil**

DIRECTIONS

1. **In a bowl toss the spinach with olive oil and lime juice**
2. **Add salt, and distribute the spinach evenly onto a cookie sheet**
3. **Bake for 30 minutes at 300 F**
4. **When ready remove from the oven and serve**

AIP BREADSTICKS

Serves: *6-8*

Prep Time: ***10*** Minutes

Cook Time: ***15*** Minutes

Total Time: 25 Minutes

INGREDIENTS

- **4 tablespoons olive oil**
- **2 tablespoons water**
- **½ cup coconut flour**
- **¼ tsp baking soda**
- **1 tsp rosemary**
- **1 tsp lemon juice**
- **1 tablespoon unflavored gelatin**
- **¼ tsp garlic powder**
- **¼ tsp salt**

DIRECTIONS

1. **Preheat oven to 325 F**
2. **In a blender add gelatin, 1 tablespoon of water, and blend**
3. **Add the rest of ingredients and blend until it thickens**
4. **Remove dough and divide into 6-8 portions**
5. **Grease each ball with olive oil and form small sticks**

6. Sprinkle garlic, salt and rosemary on each one
7. Bake at 325 F for 12-15 minutes
8. When ready remove from the oven and serve

CAULIFLOWER RICE

Serves: *4*

Prep Time: *10* Minutes

Cook Time: *15* Minutes

Total Time: *25* Minutes

INGREDIENTS

- **1 clove garlic**
- **1 tablespoon olive oil**
- **1 head cauliflower**
- **¼ cup yellow onion**
- **¼ tsp salt**
- **1 tsp herb seasoning**

DIRECTIONS

1. **Grate the cauliflower and place it in a blender**
2. **Blend until smooth**
3. **In a skillet heat coconut oil**
4. **Sauté garlic, onion and cauliflower for 4-5 minutes**
5. **Season with salt, pepper and serve**

GLAZED SALMON

Serves: 2

Prep Time: *10* Minutes

Cook Time: 25 Minutes

Total Time: 35 Minutes

INGREDIENTS

- 12 oz. salmon filet
- 1 tablespoon maple syrup
- 1 tablespoon coconut aminos
- 1 tablespoon olive oil

DIRECTIONS

1. Preheat the oven to 325 F
2. In a saucepan add maple syrup, coconut aminos and olive oil and stir until a glaze has formed
3. Place salmon filet on a baking sheet and brush with glaze
4. Bake for 20-25 minutes or until the fish is tender
5. When ready remove from heat and serve

BISON STEW

Serves: *6*

Prep Time: ***10*** Minutes

Cook Time: ***50*** Minutes

Total Time: ***60*** Minutes

INGREDIENTS

- **2 lb. bison steak**
- **1 tablespoon coconut oil**
- **2 cups celery**
- **2 sprig thyme**
- **1 head cauliflower**
- **1 onion**
- **1-quart beef broth**
- **¼ tsp salt**

DIRECTIONS

1. **In a skillet brown the stew on both sides and transfer to a pot**
2. **In the pot add celery, onion and beef broth**
3. **Add celery, thyme, cauliflower and bring to a boil**
4. **Simmer for 40-50 minutes or until the stew is completely cooked**

GARLIC AND HERB SCALLOPS

Serves: *4*

Prep Time: *10* Minutes

Cook Time: *15* Minutes

Total Time: *25* Minutes

INGREDIENTS

- **¼ cup water**
- **1 tablespoon olive oil**
- **1 tablespoon lemon juice**
- **¼ tsp salt**
- **¼ tsp onion powder**
- **¼ tsp garlic**
- **4 oz. scallops**
- **1 cup kale**
- **1 tablespoon salad dressing**

DIRECTIONS

1. **In a pot toss scallop with salad dressing**
2. **Place scallops in a steamer with all vegetables and steam for 12-15 minutes**
3. **Remove from pot and place vegetables on a plate**
4. **Add lemon juice, seasoning and serve**

ROASTED ROSEMARY BEETS

Serves: 2

Prep Time: *10* Minutes

Cook Time: *35* Minutes

Total Time: *45* Minutes

INGREDIENTS

- 2 tablespoons olive oil
- 2 tablespoons rosemary
- 2 beets
- ¼ salt

DIRECTIONS

1. Preheat the oven to 375 F
2. Brush beets with olive oil, sprinkle with salt and rosemary
3. Place the beets in a baking dish
4. Roast beets for 30-35 minutes
5. When ready remove from the oven and serve

BACON-WRAPPED SHRIMP

Serves: *8*

Prep Time: ***10*** Minutes

Cook Time: ***30*** Minutes

Total Time: ***40*** Minutes

INGREDIENTS

- 1 lb. shrimp
- 12 oz. bacon

DIRECTIONS

1. **Cut bacon in half and wrap each shrimp with bacon**
2. **Skewer each shrimp and place the skewers on a baking sheet**
3. **Cook for 25-30 minutes**
4. **When ready remove from the oven and serve**

PORK CHOPS WITH ONION

Serves: *4*

Prep Time: *10* Minutes

Cook Time: *20* Minutes

Total Time: *30* Minutes

INGREDIENTS

- **2 tablespoons lard**
- **1 lb. pork chops**
- **¼ onion**
- **1 tsp fennel**
- **¼ tsp salt**
- **Juice of 1 lemon**

DIRECTIONS

1. **In a skillet add the onions and cook until soft**
2. **Season pork chops with salt and fennel**
3. **Place the pork chops in the skillet and cook for 5-6 minutes per side**
4. **Remove pork chops from the pan and set aside**
5. **Add lemon juice, parsley and pour mixture over pork chops, serve when ready**

BACON & KALE

Serves: ***4***

Prep Time: ***5*** Minutes

Cook Time: ***10*** Minutes

Total Time: ***15*** Minutes

INGREDIENTS

- **1 bunch kale**
- **2 oz. bacon**
- **½ cup broth**
- **1 tablespoon lemon juice**
- **1 clove garlic**

DIRECTIONS

1. **Place the bacon in a skillet and cook until crispy**
2. **Add broth, kale, and cook until broth has evaporated**
3. **Add garlic, lemon juice and stir for 1-2 minutes**
4. **When ready remove and serve**

GREEK SALAD

Serves: 2
Prep Time: 5 Minutes
Cook Time: 5 Minutes
Total Time: *10* Minutes

INGREDIENTS

- **1 cup cherry tomatoes**
- **1 cucumber**
- **1 cup olives**
- **½ cup onion**
- **1 cup feta**
- **1 cup salad dressing**

DIRECTIONS

1. **In a bowl mix all ingredients and mix well**
2. **Serve with dressing**

QUINOA AND LENTIL SALAD

Serves: **2**

Prep Time: ***5*** Minutes

Cook Time: ***5*** Minutes

Total Time: ***10*** Minutes

INGREDIENTS

- **1 cup cooked lentils**
- **1 tsp salt**
- **1 cup cooked quinoa**
- **2 tablespoons olive oil**
- **1 tsp salt**
- **1 tomato**
- **1 avocado**
- **1 tsp cilantro**

DIRECTIONS

1. **In a bowl mix all ingredients and mix well**
2. **Serve with dressing**

CRANBERRY & SPINACH SALAD

Serves: 2

Prep Time: 5 Minutes

Cook Time: 5 Minutes

Total Time: *10* Minutes

INGREDIENTS

- 2 cups cooked quinoa
- 1 cup spinach leaves
- ¼ cup cranberries
- ¼ cup walnuts
- ½ avocado

DIRECTIONS

1. In a bowl mix all ingredients and mix well
2. Serve with dressing

KALE SALAD

Serves: 2

Prep Time: *5* Minutes

Cook Time: *5* Minutes

Total Time: ***10*** Minutes

INGREDIENTS

- **1 bunch kale**
- **1 cup cooked chickpeas**
- **¼ red onion**
- **¼ cup tahini**
- **¼ cup lemon juice**
- **1 cup salad dressing**

DIRECTIONS

1. **In a bowl mix all ingredients and mix well**
2. **Serve with dressing**

TORTELLINI SALAD

Serves: 2

Prep Time: 5 Minutes

Cook Time: 5 Minutes

Total Time: *10* Minutes

INGREDIENTS

- 1 lb. tortellini
- ¼ cup olive oil
- 1 tablespoon balsamic vinegar
- 1 tsp salt
- 1 cup spinach leaves
- ½ cup Parmesan
- 1 cup tomatoes

DIRECTIONS

1. **In a bowl mix all ingredients and mix well**
2. **Serve with dressing**

TACO SALAD

Serves: 2

Prep Time: *5* Minutes

Cook Time: *5* Minutes

Total Time: ***10*** Minutes

INGREDIENTS

- **½ cup olive oil**
- **1 lb. cooked steak**
- **1 tablespoon taco seasoning**
- **Juice of 1 lime**
- **1 tsp cumin**
- **1 head romaine lettuce**
- **1 cup corn**
- **1 cup beans**
- **1 cup tomatoes**

DIRECTIONS

1. **In a bowl mix all ingredients and mix well**
2. **Serve with dressing**

DORITO TACO SALAD

Serves: 2
Prep Time: 5 Minutes

Cook Time: 5 Minutes

Total Time: *10* Minutes

INGREDIENTS

- **1 lb. cooked beef**
- **1 tsp chili powder**
- **1 tsp paprika**
- **1 tsp cumin**
- **1 head romaine lettuce**
- **1 cup cherry tomatoes**
- **1 cup cheddar cheese**
- **1 avocado**
- **1 bag doritos**
- **¼ cup sour cream**

DIRECTIONS

1. **In a bowl mix all ingredients and mix well**
2. **Serve with dressing**

CHEESEBURGER SALAD

Serves: 2
Prep Time: 5 Minutes

Cook Time: 5 Minutes

Total Time: *10* Minutes

INGREDIENTS

- **1 lb. cooked beef**
- **1 tsp garlic powder**
- **1 tsp Worcestershire sauce**
- **1 tsp black pepper**
- **1 cup salad dressing**
- **1 head romaine lettuce**
- **1 cup cheddar cheese**
- **1/4 red onion**
- **1 tsp sesame seeds**

DIRECTIONS

1. **In a bowl mix all ingredients and mix well**
2. **Serve with dressing**

MANDARIN SALAD

Serves: 2

Prep Time: 5 Minutes

Cook Time: 5 Minutes

Total Time: *10* Minutes

INGREDIENTS

- **2 cups lettuce**
- **2 cups red cabbage**
- **2 cups cooked chicken**
- **¼ cup carrot**
- **¼ cup almonds**

DRESSING

- **1 tablespoon honey**
- **2 tablespoons rice wine vinegar**
- **1 tablespoon soy sauce**
- **1 tablespoon hoisin sauce**

DIRECTIONS

1. **In a bowl mix all ingredients and mix well**
2. **Serve with dressing**

SOUTHWESTERN SALAD

Serves: 2

Prep Time: *5* Minutes

Cook Time: *5* Minutes

Total Time: ***10*** Minutes

INGREDIENTS

- **1 lb. cooked penne**
- **1 can corn kernels**
- **1 can beans**
- **1 cup cheddar cheese**
- **1 avocado**
- **½ cup cilantro**
- **1 cup salad dressing**

DIRECTIONS

1. **In a bowl mix all ingredients and mix well**
2. **Serve with dressing**

BUTTERNUT SQUASH STEW

Serves: *4*

Prep Time: *15* Minutes

Cook Time: *45* Minutes

Total Time: *60* Minutes

INGREDIENTS

- **2 tablespoons olive oil**
- **2 red onions**
- **2 cloves garlic**
- **1. Tablespoon rosemary**
- **1 tablespoon thyme**
- **2 lb. beef**
- **1 cup white wine**
- **1 cup butternut squash**
- **2 cups beef broth**
- **½ cup tomatoes**

DIRECTIONS

1. **Chop all ingredients in big chunks**
2. **In a large pot heat olive oil and add ingredients one by one**
3. **Cook for 5-6 or until slightly brown**

4. **Add remaining ingredients and cook until tender, 35-45 minutes**
5. **Season while stirring on low heat**
6. **When ready remove from heat and serve**

BEEF STEW

Serves: *4*

Prep Time: *15* Minutes

Cook Time: *45* Minutes

Total Time: *60* Minutes

INGREDIENTS

- 2 lb. beef
- 1 tsp salt
- 4 tablespoons olive oil
- 2 red onions
- 2 cloves garlic
- 1 cup white wine
- 2 cups beef broth
- 1 cup water
- 3-4 bay leaves
- ¼ tsp thyme
- 1 lb. potatoes

DIRECTIONS

1. Chop all ingredients in big chunks
2. In a large pot heat olive oil and add ingredients one by one
3. Cook for 5-6 or until slightly brown

4. **Add remaining ingredients and cook until tender, 35-45 minutes**
5. **Season while stirring on low heat**
6. **When ready remove from heat and serve**

CORN CASSEROLE

Serves: ***4***

Prep Time: ***10*** Minutes

Cook Time: ***15*** Minutes

Total Time: ***25*** Minutes

INGREDIENTS

- ½ cup cornmeal
- ½ cup butter
- 2 eggs
- 1 cup milk
- ½ cup heavy cream
- 3 cups corn
- ¼ tsp smoked paprika

DIRECTIONS

1. **Sauté the veggies and set aside**
2. **Preheat the oven to 425 F**
3. **Transfer the sautéed veggies to a baking dish, add remaining ingredients to the baking dish**
4. **Mix well, add seasoning and place the dish in the oven**
5. **Bake for 12-15 minutes or until slightly brown**

6. **When ready remove from the oven and serve**

ARTICHOKE CASSEROLE

Serves: *4*

Prep Time: *10* Minutes

Cook Time: *15* Minutes

Total Time: *25* Minutes

INGREDIENTS

- 1 cup cooked rice
- 1 cup milk
- 1 cup parmesan cheese
- 4 oz. cream cheese
- 1 lb. cooked chicken breast
- 1 cup spinach
- 1 can artichoke hearts
- 1 cup mozzarella cheese

DIRECTIONS

1. Sauté the veggies and set aside
2. Preheat the oven to 425 F
3. Transfer the sautéed veggies to a baking dish, add remaining ingredients to the baking dish
4. Mix well, add seasoning and place the dish in the oven
5. Bake for 12-15 minutes or until slightly brown
6. When ready remove from the oven and serve

PIZZA RECIPES

MUSHROOM PIZZA

Serves: 2

Prep Time: ***10*** Minutes

Cook Time: ***30*** Minutes

Total Time: ***40*** Minutes

INGREDIENTS

- **2 button mushrooms**
- **½ red onion**
- **1 lemon juiced**
- **1 tablespoon parsley**
- **½ cup ground flax seeds**
- **2 tablespoons olive oil**
- **1 cup almonds whole**
- **1 cup cashews whole**
- **1 carrot**

DIRECTIONS

1. **Preheat oven to 375 F and place a baking sheet**
2. **In food processor place all the ingredients and blend for 8-10 minutes**

3. **Pour the mixture on the baking sheet and bake for 15-20 minutes until golden**
4. **Remove from the oven and serve**

CASSEROLE PIZZA

Serves: *6-8*

Prep Time: ***10*** Minutes

Cook Time: *15* Minutes

Total Time: *25* Minutes

INGREDIENTS

- **1 pizza crust**
- **½ cup tomato sauce**
- **¼ black pepper**
- **1 cup zucchini slices**
- **1 cup mozzarella cheese**
- **1 cup olives**

DIRECTIONS

1. **Spread tomato sauce on the pizza crust**
2. **Place all the toppings on the pizza crust**
3. **Bake the pizza at 425 F for 12-15 minutes**
4. **When ready remove pizza from the oven and serve**

SEVENTH COOKBOOK

BLUEBERRY PANCAKES

Serves: ***4***

Prep Time: ***10*** Minutes

Cook Time: ***20*** Minutes

Total Time: ***30*** Minutes

INGREDIENTS

- **1 cup whole wheat flour**
- **¼ tsp baking soda**
- **¼ tsp baking powder**
- **1 cup blueberries**
- **2 eggs**
- **1 cup milk**

DIRECTIONS

1. **In a bowl combine all ingredients together and mix well**
2. **In a skillet heat olive oil**
3. **Pour ¼ of the batter and cook each pancake for 1-2 minutes per side**
4. **When ready remove from heat and serve**

NECTARINE PANCAKES

Serves: ***4***

Prep Time: ***10*** Minutes

Cook Time: ***30*** Minutes

Total Time: ***40*** Minutes

INGREDIENTS

- **1 cup whole wheat flour**
- **¼ tsp baking soda**
- **¼ tsp baking powder**
- **1 cup nectarine**
- **2 eggs**
- **1 cup milk**

DIRECTIONS

1. **In a bowl combine all ingredients together and mix well**
2. **In a skillet heat olive oil**
3. **Pour ¼ of the batter and cook each pancake for 1-2 minutes per side**
4. **When ready remove from heat and serve**

BANANA PANCAKES

Serves: *4*

Prep Time: *10* Minutes

Cook Time: *20* Minutes

Total Time: *30* Minutes

INGREDIENTS

- **1 cup whole wheat flour**
- **¼ tsp baking soda**
- **¼ tsp baking powder**
- **1 cup mashed banana**
- **2 eggs**
- **1 cup milk**

DIRECTIONS

1. **In a bowl combine all ingredients together and mix well**
2. **In a skillet heat olive oil**
3. **Pour ¼ of the batter and cook each pancake for 1-2 minutes per side**
4. **When ready remove from heat and serve**

ONION PANCAKES

Serves: *4*

Prep Time: *10* Minutes

Cook Time: *20* Minutes

Total Time: *30* Minutes

INGREDIENTS

- 1 cup whole wheat flour
- ¼ tsp baking soda
- ¼ tsp baking powder
- 1 cup onion
- 2 eggs
- 1 cup milk

DIRECTIONS

1. In a bowl combine all ingredients together and mix well
2. In a skillet heat olive oil
3. Pour ¼ of the batter and cook each pancake for 1-2 minutes per side
4. When ready remove from heat and serve

PANCAKES

Serves: ***4***

Prep Time: ***10*** Minutes

Cook Time: ***30*** Minutes

Total Time: ***40*** Minutes

INGREDIENTS

- **1 cup whole wheat flour**
- **¼ tsp baking soda**
- **¼ tsp baking powder**
- **2 eggs**
- **1 cup milk**

DIRECTIONS

1. **In a bowl combine all ingredients together and mix well**
2. **In a skillet heat olive oil**
3. **Pour ¼ of the batter and cook each pancake for 1-2 minutes per side**
4. **When ready remove from heat and serve**

MANDARIN MUFFINS

Serves: *8-12*

Prep Time: ***10*** Minutes

Cook Time: ***20*** Minutes

Total Time: ***30*** Minutes

INGREDIENTS

- **2 eggs**
- **1 tablespoon olive oil**
- **1 cup milk**
- **2 cups whole wheat flour**
- **1 tsp baking soda**
- **¼ tsp baking soda**
- **1 tsp ginger**
- **1 cup mandarin**
- **¼ cup molasses**

DIRECTIONS

1. **In a bowl combine all wet ingredients**
2. **In another bowl combine all dry ingredients**
3. **Combine wet and dry ingredients together**
4. **Pour mixture into 8-12 prepared muffin cups, fill 2/3 of the cups**
5. **Bake for 18-20 minutes at 375 F, when ready remove and serve**

BANANA MUFFINS

Serves: *8-12*

Prep Time: ***10*** Minutes

Cook Time: ***20*** Minutes

Total Time: ***30*** Minutes

INGREDIENTS

- **2 eggs**
- **1 tablespoon olive oil**
- **1 cup milk**
- **2 cups whole wheat flour**
- **1 tsp baking soda**
- **¼ tsp baking soda**
- **1 tsp cinnamon**
- **1 cup mashed banana**

DIRECTIONS

1. **In a bowl combine all wet ingredients**
2. **In another bowl combine all dry ingredients**
3. **Combine wet and dry ingredients together**
4. **Fold in mashed banana and mix well**
5. **Pour mixture into 8-12 prepared muffin cups, fill 2/3 of the cups**
6. **Bake for 18-20 minutes at 375 F, when ready remove and serve**

POMEGRANATE MUFFINS

Serves: *8-12*

Prep Time: *10* Minutes

Cook Time: *20* Minutes

Total Time: *30* Minutes

INGREDIENTS

- 2 eggs
- 1 tablespoon olive oil
- 1 cup milk
- 2 cups whole wheat flour
- 1 tsp baking soda
- ¼ tsp baking soda
- 1 tsp cinnamon
- 1 cup pomegranate

DIRECTIONS

1. In a bowl combine all wet ingredients
2. In another bowl combine all dry ingredients
3. Combine wet and dry ingredients together
4. Pour mixture into 8-12 prepared muffin cups, fill 2/3 of the cups
5. Bake for 18-20 minutes at 375 F
6. When ready remove from the oven and serve

STRAWBERRY MUFFINS

Serves: *8-12*

Prep Time: ***10*** Minutes

Cook Time: ***20*** Minutes

Total Time: ***30*** Minutes

INGREDIENTS

- 2 eggs
- 1 tablespoon olive oil
- 1 cup milk
- 2 cups whole wheat flour
- 1 tsp baking soda
- ¼ tsp baking soda
- 1 tsp cinnamon
- 1 cup strawberries

DIRECTIONS

1. In a bowl combine all wet ingredients
2. In another bowl combine all dry ingredients
3. Combine wet and dry ingredients together
4. Fold in strawberries and mix well
5. Pour mixture into 8-12 prepared muffin cups, fill 2/3 of the cups
6. Bake for 18-20 minutes at 375 F, when ready remove and serve

PLUMS MUFFINS

Serves: *8-12*

Prep Time: ***10*** Minutes

Cook Time: ***20*** Minutes

Total Time: ***30*** Minutes

INGREDIENTS

- 2 eggs
- 1 tablespoon olive oil
- 1 cup milk
- 2 cups whole wheat flour
- 1 tsp baking soda
- ¼ tsp baking soda
- 1 tsp cinnamon
- 1 cup plums

DIRECTIONS

1. In a bowl combine all wet ingredients
2. In another bowl combine all dry ingredients
3. Combine wet and dry ingredients together
4. Pour mixture into 8-12 prepared muffin cups, fill 2/3 of the cups
5. Bake for 18-20 minutes at 375 F
6. When ready remove from the oven and serve

MUFFINS

Serves: *8-12*

Prep Time: ***10*** Minutes

Cook Time: ***20*** Minutes

Total Time: ***30*** Minutes

INGREDIENTS

- 2 eggs
- 1 tablespoon olive oil
- 1 cup milk
- 2 cups whole wheat flour
- 1 tsp baking soda
- ¼ tsp baking soda
- 1 tsp cinnamon

DIRECTIONS

1. In a bowl combine all wet ingredients
2. In another bowl combine all dry ingredients
3. Combine wet and dry ingredients together
4. Pour mixture into 8-12 prepared muffin cups, fill 2/3 of the cups
5. Bake for 18-20 minutes at 375 F
6. When ready remove from the oven and serve

POTATO OMELETTE

Serves: *1*

Prep Time: 5 Minutes

Cook Time: *10* Minutes

Total Time: *15* Minutes

INGREDIENTS

- **2 eggs**
- **¼ tsp salt**
- **¼ tsp black pepper**
- **1 tablespoon olive oil**
- **¼ cup cheese**
- **½ lb. sweet potato**
- **¼ tsp basil**

DIRECTIONS

1. **In a bowl combine all ingredients together and mix well**
2. **In a skillet heat olive oil and pour the egg mixture**
3. **Cook for 1-2 minutes per side**
4. **When ready remove omelette from the skillet and serve**

ZUCCHINI OMELETTE

Serves: *1*

Prep Time: *5* Minutes

Cook Time: *10* Minutes

Total Time: *15* Minutes

INGREDIENTS

- 2 eggs
- ¼ tsp salt
- ¼ tsp black pepper
- 1 tablespoon olive oil
- ¼ cup cheese
- ¼ tsp basil
- 1 cup zucchini

DIRECTIONS

1. In a bowl combine all ingredients together and mix well
2. In a skillet heat olive oil and pour the egg mixture
3. Cook for 1-2 minutes per side
4. When ready remove omelette from the skillet and serve

BASIL OMELETTE

Serves: *1*

Prep Time: *5* Minutes

Cook Time: *10* Minutes

Total Time: *15* Minutes

INGREDIENTS

- **2 eggs**
- **¼ tsp salt**
- **¼ tsp black pepper**
- **1 tablespoon olive oil**
- **¼ cup cheese**
- **¼ tsp basil**
- **1 cup red onion**

DIRECTIONS

1. **In a bowl combine all ingredients together and mix well**
2. **In a skillet heat olive oil and pour the egg mixture**
3. **Cook for 1-2 minutes per side**
4. **When ready remove omelette from the skillet and serve**

MUSHROOM OMELETTE

Serves: *1*

Prep Time: *5* Minutes

Cook Time: *10* Minutes

Total Time: *15* Minutes

INGREDIENTS

- 2 eggs
- ¼ tsp salt
- ¼ tsp black pepper
- 1 tablespoon olive oil
- ¼ cup cheese
- ¼ tsp basil
- 1 cup mushrooms

DIRECTIONS

1. In a bowl combine all ingredients together and mix well
2. In a skillet heat olive oil and pour the egg mixture
3. Cook for 1-2 minutes per side
4. When ready remove omelette from the skillet and serve

PUMPKIN OMELETTE

Serves: *1*

Prep Time: *5* Minutes

Cook Time: *10* Minutes

Total Time: *15* Minutes

INGREDIENTS

- **2 eggs**
- **¼ tsp salt**
- **¼ tsp black pepper**
- **1 tablespoon olive oil**
- **¼ cup cheese**
- **¼ tsp basil**
- **1 cup pumpkin puree**

DIRECTIONS

1. **In a bowl combine all ingredients together and mix well**
2. **In a skillet heat olive oil and pour the egg mixture**
3. **Cook for 1-2 minutes per side**
4. **When ready remove omelette from the skillet and serve**

BLUEBERRIES OATMEAL

Serves: 2
Prep Time: *10* Minutes
Cook Time: *8* Hours
Total Time: *8* Hours

INGREDIENTS

- **1/3 cup oats**
- **1/3 cup blueberries**
- **2 tbs maple syrup**
- **1/3 cup coconut milk**
- **½ tsp vanilla**
- **1 banana**
- **1 ½ tsp chia seeds**

DIRECTIONS

1. **Mix the oats and chia seeds together**
2. **Pour in the milk and top with blueberries and sliced banana**
3. **Refrigerate for at least 8 hours**
4. **Stir in the maple syrup and serve**

CHIA PUDDING

Serves: 2
Prep Time: 5 Minutes

Cook Time: *10* Minutes

Total Time: *15* Minutes

INGREDIENTS

- **5 tbs chia seeds**
- **1 ½ tbs vanilla**
- **2 tbs maple syrup**
- **2 ½ cup almond milk**
- **1 ½ cup strawberries**
- **1 beet**

DIRECTIONS

1. **Blend together the milk, strawberries, chopped beet, maple syrup, and vanilla**
2. **Pour into a cup and ad the chia**
3. **Stir every 5 minutes for 15 minutes**
4. **Refrigerate overnight**
5. **Serve topped with fruits**

BREAKFAST CASSEROLE

Serves: ***4***

Prep Time: ***10*** Minutes

Cook Time: *35* Minutes

Total Time: *45* Minutes

INGREDIENTS

- **7 oz asparagus**
- **3 tbs parsley**
- **1 cup broccoli**
- **1 zucchini**
- **3 tbs oil**
- **5 eggs**
- **Salt**
- **Pepper**

DIRECTIONS

1. **Cook the diced zucchini, asparagus and broccoli florets in heated oil for about 5 minutes**
2. **Season with salt and pepper and remove from heat**
3. **Whisk the eggs and season then add the parsley**
4. **Place the vegetables in a greased pan then pour the eggs over**
5. **Bake in the preheated oven for about 35 minutes at 350F**

BLUEBERRY BALLS

Serves: *12*

Prep Time: *5* Minutes

Cook Time: *30* Minutes

Total Time: *35* Minutes

INGREDIENTS

- **2 cups oats**
- **1 cup blueberries**
- **1/3 cup honey**
- **1 tsp cinnamon**
- **1 ½ tsp vanilla**
- **1/3 cup almond butter**

DIRECTIONS

1. **Mix the honey, vanilla, oats, almond butter, and cinnamon together**
2. **Fold in the blueberries**
3. **Refrigerate for at least 30 minutes**
4. **Form balls from the dough and serve**

ZUCCHINI BREAD

Serves: ***4***

Prep Time: ***10*** Minutes

Cook Time: ***40*** Minutes

Total Time: ***50*** Minutes

INGREDIENTS

- **4 tbs honey**
- **5 tbs oil**
- **1 ½ tsp baking soda**
- **3 eggs**
- **½ cup walnuts**
- **2 ½ cups flour**
- **4 Medjool dates**
- **1 banana**
- **2 tsp mixed spice**
- **1 ½ cup zucchini**

DIRECTIONS

1. **Preheat the oven to 350 F**
2. **Chop the dates and the walnuts**
3. **Mix the flour, spice and baking soda together**
4. **Mix the eggs and banana in a food processor then add remaining ingredients and mix**

5. Pour the batter into a pan and cook for at least 40 minutes
6. Allow to cool then serve

LUNCH

TOMATO FRITATTA

Serves: **2**

Prep Time: ***10*** Minutes

Cook Time: ***20*** Minutes

Total Time: ***30*** Minutes

INGREDIENTS

- **½ lb. tomato**
- **1 tablespoon olive oil**
- **½ red onion**
- **¼ tsp salt**
- **2 eggs**
- **2 oz. cheddar cheese**
- **1 garlic clove**
- **¼ tsp dill**

DIRECTIONS

1. **In a bowl whisk eggs with salt and cheese**
2. **In a frying pan heat olive oil and pour egg mixture**
3. **Add remaining ingredients and mix well**
4. **Serve when ready**

YAM ROOT FRITATTA

Serves: 2

Prep Time: *10* Minutes

Cook Time: *20* Minutes

Total Time: *30* Minutes

INGREDIENTS

- **½ cup yam root**
- **1 tablespoon olive oil**
- **½ red onion**
- **¼ tsp salt**
- **2 eggs**
- **2 oz. cheddar cheese**
- **1 garlic clove**
- **¼ tsp dill**

DIRECTIONS

1. **In a bowl whisk eggs with salt and cheese**
2. **In a frying pan heat olive oil and pour egg mixture**
3. **Add remaining ingredients and mix well**
4. **Serve when ready**

WATERCRESS FRITATTA

Serves: *2*

Prep Time: *10* Minutes

Cook Time: *20* Minutes

Total Time: *30* Minutes

INGREDIENTS

- **1 cup watercress**
- **1 tablespoon olive oil**
- **½ red onion**
- **¼ tsp salt**
- **2 eggs**
- **2 oz. cheddar cheese**
- **1 garlic clove**
- **¼ tsp dill**

DIRECTIONS

1. **In a bowl whisk eggs with salt and cheese**
2. **In a frying pan heat olive oil and pour egg mixture**
3. **Add remaining ingredients and mix well**
4. **Serve when ready**

ZUCCHINI FRITATTA

Serves: 2

Prep Time: *10* Minutes

Cook Time: *20* Minutes

Total Time: *30* Minutes

INGREDIENTS

- **1 cup zucchini**
- **1 tablespoon olive oil**
- **½ red onion**
- **¼ tsp salt**
- **2 eggs**
- **2 oz. parmesan cheese**
- **1 garlic clove**
- **¼ tsp dill**

DIRECTIONS

1. **In a skillet sauté zucchini until tender**
2. **In a bowl whisk eggs with salt and cheese**
3. **In a frying pan heat olive oil and pour egg mixture**
4. **Add remaining ingredients and mix well**
5. **Serve when ready**

BROCCOLI FRITATTA

Serves: 2

Prep Time: *10* Minutes

Cook Time: *20* Minutes

Total Time: *30* Minutes

INGREDIENTS

- 1 cup broccoli
- 1 tablespoon olive oil
- ½ red onion
- ¼ tsp salt
- 2 eggs
- 2 oz. cheddar cheese
- 1 garlic clove
- ¼ tsp dill

DIRECTIONS

1. In a skillet sauté broccoli until tender
2. In a bowl whisk eggs with salt and cheese
3. In a frying pan heat olive oil and pour egg mixture
4. Add remaining ingredients and mix well
5. Serve when ready

MOZZARELLA STUFFED CHICKEN BREAST

Serves: 2

Prep Time: *10* Minutes

Cook Time: *25* Minutes

Total Time: *35* Minutes

INGREDIENTS

- **2 chicken breasts**
- **1 tsp salt**
- **6-7 asparagus spears**
- **½ cup mozzarella cheese**
- **2 tsp olive oil**
- **½ cup bread crumbs**

DIRECTIONS

1. **Drizzle olive oil and salt over the chicken breast**
2. **Place the chicken breast in the breadcrumbs bowl and toss well**
3. **Cut the chicken breast and stuff mozzarella inside**
4. **Roast chicken breast with asparagus at 400 F for 20-25 minutes**
5. **When ready remove from the oven and serve**

MACARONI AND CHEESE

Serves: 2

Prep Time: *10* Minutes

Cook Time: *20* Minutes

Total Time: *30* Minutes

INGREDIENTS

- **1 cup macaroni**
- **1 tablespoon olive oil**
- **1 tablespoon all-purpose flour**
- **1 tsp salt**
- **1 tsp garlic powder**
- **1 cup milk**
- **1 cup mozzarella cheese**
- **½ cup parmesan cheese**

DIRECTIONS

1. **In a skillet heat olive oil, stir in flour, garlic, salt, milk and cook on low heat**
2. **Add mozzarella, macaroni and mix well**
3. **When ready remove from heat and serve with parmesan cheese on top**

BUTTERNUT SQUASH BISQUE

Serves: *4*

Prep Time: *10* Minutes

Cook Time: *30* Minutes

Total Time: *40* Minutes

INGREDIENTS

- **1 tablespoon olive oil**
- **¼ cup red onion**
- **½ cup carrots**
- **4 cups butternut squash**
- **2 cups vegetable stock**
- **1 tsp salt**

DIRECTIONS

1. **In a pot heat olive oil, add onion and cook until tender**
2. **Add squash and carrots to the pot**
3. **Add vegetable stock, salt and bring to a boil**
4. **Simmer on low heat until vegetables are tender**
5. **Blend the soup until smooth, return to the pot and cook for another 5-10 minutes**
6. **When ready remove from heat and serve**

GARLIC CHICKEN

Serves: 2

Prep Time: *10* Minutes

Cook Time: *40* Minutes

Total Time: *50* Minutes

INGREDIENTS

- **2 tablespoons butter**
- **1 tablespoon garlic powder**
- **1 tsp rosemary**
- **1 tsp salt**
- **1 cup honey**
- **4 chicken thighs**

DIRECTIONS

1. **In a saucepan melt butter, add garlic, rosemary, salt and simmer on low heat for 30-60 seconds**
2. **Add honey and dip the chicken into the mixture**
3. **Cook for 2-3 minutes, be sure to be well coated**
4. **Transfer to the oven and bake at 400 F for 30-35 minutes**
5. **When ready remove from the oven and serve**

PASTA WITH CREAM SAUCE

Serves: 2

Prep Time: *10* Minutes

Cook Time: *30* Minutes

Total Time: *40* Minutes

INGREDIENTS

- **2 cups penne pasta**
- **2 tablespoons butter**
- **1 lb. chicken breast**
- **1 tsp garlic**
- **1 cup canned pumpkin**
- **¼ cup heavy cream**
- **1 tablespoon sage leaves**
- **¼ tsp salt**
- **¼ cup pecans**

DIRECTIONS

1. **Cook pasta and set aside**
2. **In a skillet melt butter, add garlic, chicken and cook on medium heat until chicken is cooked**
3. **Add pasta, pumpkin, heavy cream, sage, salt and pecans**
4. **Toss to coat and cook on low heat for 5-10 minutes**
5. **When ready remove from the pot and serve**

ROASTED SALAD

Serves: 2
Prep Time: 5 Minutes

Cook Time: 5 Minutes

Total Time: *10* Minutes

INGREDIENTS

- **1 cup cauliflower**
- **1 cup broccoli**
- **1 cup brussels sprouts**
- **1 cup red bell pepper**
- **1 cup squash**
- **1 tablespoon olive oil**

DIRECTIONS

1. **In a bowl combine all ingredients together and mix well**
2. **Serve with dressing**

PUMPKIN SALAD

Serves: 2

Prep Time: 5 Minutes

Cook Time: 5 Minutes

Total Time: *10* Minutes

INGREDIENTS

- **½ cauliflower florets**
- **1 cup pumpkin**
- **1 cup Brussel sprouts**
- **1 cup quinoa**
- **1 tablespoon olive oil**

DIRECTIONS

1. **In a bowl combine all ingredients together and mix well**
2. **Serve with dressing**

DUCK SALAD

Serves: 2

Prep Time: *5* Minutes

Cook Time: *5* Minutes

Total Time: ***10*** Minutes

INGREDIENTS

- **1 cooked duck breast**
- **½ lb. Brussel sprouts**
- **1 cup broccoli florets**
- **1 apple**
- **3 oz. blueberries**
- **1 tsp olive oil**
- **1 cup blueberry salad dressing**

DIRECTIONS

1. **In a bowl combine all ingredients together and mix well**
2. **Serve with dressing**

BRUSSELS SPROUT SALAD

Serves: 2

Prep Time: 5 Minutes

Cook Time: 5 Minutes

Total Time: *10* Minutes

INGREDIENTS

- ½ lb. Brussels sprouts
- 1 cup cauliflower florets
- ½ lb. carrot
- 2 oz. lettuce
- 3 oz. cooked breast chicken
- 1 tsp olive oil

DIRECTIONS

1. In a bowl combine all ingredients together and mix well
2. Serve with dressing

ANTI-INFLAMMATORY SALAD

Serves: 2
Prep Time: *5* Minutes

Cook Time: *5* Minutes

Total Time: ***10*** Minutes

INGREDIENTS

- **1 tablespoon olive oil**
- **1 tablespoon apple cider vinegar**
- **1 tablespoon lemon juice**
- **1 tsp turmeric**
- **1 clove garlic**
- **1 tsp salt**

DIRECTIONS

1. **In a bowl combine all ingredients together and mix well**
2. **Serve with dressing**

RED CHICORY SALAD

Serves: 2

Prep Time: 5 Minutes

Cook Time: 5 Minutes

Total Time: *10* Minutes

INGREDIENTS

- 2 red chicory
- 2 fennel bulbs
- ½ cup watercress
- 2 garlic cloves
- 1 tablespoon olive oil

DIRECTIONS

1. In a bowl combine all ingredients together and mix well
2. Serve with dressing

FENNEL SALAD

Serves: 2
Prep Time: *5* Minutes
Cook Time: *5* Minutes
Total Time: ***10*** Minutes

INGREDIENTS

- **1 fennel bulb**
- **1 tablespoon lemon juice**
- **¼ cup olive oil**
- **1 tsp mint**
- **1 tsp onion**

DIRECTIONS

1. **In a bowl combine all ingredients together and mix well**
2. **Serve with dressing**

GIGNER CILANTRO SALAD

Serves: 2
Prep Time: *5* Minutes

Cook Time: *5* Minutes

Total Time: ***10*** Minutes

INGREDIENTS

- **2 lb. sweet potatoes**
- **¼ cup olive oil**
- **2 tablespoons lemon juice**
- **¼ cup scallions**
- **¼ cup cilantro**
- **¼ tsp salt**

DIRECTIONS

1. **In a bowl combine all ingredients together and mix well**
2. **Serve with dressing**

CHEESE MACARONI

Serves: *1*

Prep Time: *10* Minutes

Cook Time: *20* Minutes

Total Time: *30* Minutes

INGREDIENTS

- 1 lb. macaroni
- 1 cup cheddar cheese
- 1 cup Monterey Jack cheese
- 1 cup mozzarella cheese
- ¼ tsp salt
- ¼ tsp pepper

DIRECTIONS

1. In a pot bring water to a boil
2. Add pasta and cook until al dente
3. In a bowl combine all cheese together and add it to the pasta
4. When ready transfer to a bowl, add salt, pepper and serve

POTATO CASSEROLE

Serves: 2

Prep Time: *10* Minutes

Cook Time: *20* Minutes

Total Time: *30* Minutes

INGREDIENTS

- **5-6 large potatoes**
- **¼ cup sour cream**
- **½ cup butter**
- **5-6 bacon strips**
- **1-2 cups mozzarella cheese**
- **¼ cup heavy cream**

DIRECTIONS

1. **Place the potatoes in a pot with boiling water, cook until tender**
2. **Place the potatoes in a bowl, add sour cream, butter, cheese and mix well**
3. **In a baking dish place the bacon strips and cover with potato mixture**
4. **Add remaining mozzarella cheese on top**
5. **Bake at 325 F for 15-18 minutes or until the mozzarella is fully melted**
6. **When ready remove from the oven and serve**

CHEESE STUFFED SHELLS

Serves: 2

Prep Time: *10* Minutes

Cook Time: *30* Minutes

Total Time: *40* Minutes

INGREDIENTS

- 2-3 cups macaroni
- 2 cups cream cheese
- 1 cup spaghetti sauce
- 1 cup onions
- 1 cup mozzarella cheese

DIRECTIONS

1. In a pot boil water and add shells
2. Cook for 12-15 minutes
3. In a baking dish add spaghetti sauce
4. In a bowl combine cream cheese, onion and set aside
5. Add cream cheese to the shells and place them into the baking dish
6. Bake at 325 F for 30 minutes or until golden brown
7. When ready remove from the oven and serve

POTATO SOUP

Serves: ***4-6***

Prep Time: ***10*** Minutes

Cook Time: ***50*** Minutes

Total Time: ***60*** Minutes

INGREDIENTS

- **1 onion**
- **2-3 carrots**
- **2 tablespoons flour**
- **5-6 large potatoes**
- **2 cups milk**
- **2 cups bouillon**
- **1 cup water**
- **2 cups milk**
- **1 tsp salt**
- **1 tsp pepper**

DIRECTIONS

1. **In a saucepan melt butter and sauce carrots, garlic and onion fo: 4-5 minutes**
2. **Add flour, milk, potatoes, bouillon and cook for another 15-20 minutes**

3. Add pepper and remaining ingredients and cook on low heat for 20-30 minutes
4. When ready remove from heat and serve

CHICKEN ALFREDO

Serves: 2

Prep Time: *10* Minutes

Cook Time: *20* Minutes

Total Time: *30* Minutes

INGREDIENTS

- 2-3 chicken breasts
- 1 lb. rotini
- 1 cup parmesan cheese
- 1 cup olive oil
- 1 tsp salt
- 1 tsp black pepper
- 1 tsp parsley

DIRECTIONS

1. In a pot add the rotini and cook on low heat for 12-15 minutes
2. In a frying pan heat olive oil, add chicken, salt, parsley, and cook until the chicken is brown
3. Drain the rotini and place the rotini in pan with chicken
4. Cook for 2-3 minutes

5. **When ready remove from heat and serve with parmesan cheese on top**

BUTTERNUT SQUASH PIZZA

Serves: *4-6*

Prep Time: *10* Minutes

Cook Time: *15* Minutes

Total Time: *25* Minutes

INGREDIENTS

- **2 cups butternut squash**
- **¼ tsp salt**
- **1 pizza crust**
- **5-6 tablespoons alfredo sauce**
- **1 tsp olive oil**
- **4-5 cups baby spinach**
- **2-3 oz. goat cheese**

DIRECTIONS

1. **Place the pizza crust on a baking dish and spread the alfredo sauce**
2. **In a skillet sauté spinach and place it over the pizza crust**
3. **Add goat cheese, butternut squash, olive oil and salt**
4. **Bake pizza at 425 F for 8-10 minutes**
5. **When ready remove from the oven and serve**

PENNE WITH ASPARAGUS

Serves: *2*

Prep Time: *10* Minutes

Cook Time: *20* Minutes

Total Time: *30* Minutes

INGREDIENTS

- 6-7 oz. penne pasta
- 2-3 bacon slices
- ¼ cup red onion
- 2 cups asparagus
- 1 cup chicken broth
- 2-3 cups spinach leaves
- ¼ cup parmesan cheese

DIRECTIONS

1. Cook pasta until al dente
2. In a skillet cook bacon until crispy and set aside
3. In a pan add onion, asparagus, broth and cook on low heat for 5-10 minutes
4. Add spinach, cheese, pepper, pasta and cook for another 5-6 minutes
5. When ready sprinkle bacon and serve

NOODLE SOUP

Serves: *4*

Prep Time: *10* Minutes

Cook Time: *20* Minutes

Total Time: *30* Minutes

INGREDIENTS

- **2-3 cups water**
- **1 can chicken broth**
- **1 tablespoon olive oil**
- **¼ red onion**
- **¼ cup celery**
- **¼ tsp salt**
- **¼ tsp black pepper**
- **5-6 oz. fusilli pasta**
- **2 cups chicken breast**
- **2 tablespoons parsley**

DIRECTIONS

1. **In a pot boil water with broth**
2. **In a saucepan heat oil, add carrot, pepper, celery, onion, salt and sauté until tender**
3. **Add broth mixture to the mixture and pasta**

4. **Cook until al dente and stir in chicken breast, cook until chicken breast is tender**
5. **When ready remove from heat, stir in parsley and serve**

TOMATO WRAP

Serves: *4*

Prep Time: *5* Minutes

Cook Time: *15* Minutes

Total Time: *20* Minutes

INGREDIENTS

- **1 cup corn**
- **1 cup tomatoes**
- **1 cup pickles**
- **1 tablespoon olive oil**
- **1 tablespoon mayonnaise**
- **6-7 turkey slices**
- **2-3 whole-wheat tortillas**
- **1 cup romaine lettuce**

DIRECTIONS

1. **In a bowl combine tomatoes, pickles, olive oil, corn and set aside**
2. **Place the turkey slices over the tortillas and top with tomato mixture and mayonnaise**
3. **Roll and serve**

THYME COD

Serves: 2

Prep Time: *5* Minutes

Cook Time: *15* Minutes

Total Time: *20* Minutes

INGREDIENTS

- **1 tablespoon olive oil**
- **½ red onion**
- **1 can tomatoes**
- **2-3 springs thyme**
- **2-3 cod fillets**

DIRECTIONS

1. **In a frying pan heat olive oil and sauté onion, stir in tomatoes, spring thyme and cook for 5-6 minutes**
2. **Add cod fillets, cover and cook for 5-6 minutes per side**
3. **When ready remove from heat and serve**

VEGGIE STIR-FRY

Serves: 2
Prep Time: *10* Minutes

Cook Time: *20* Minutes

Total Time: *30* Minutes

INGREDIENTS

- 1 tablespoon cornstarch
- 1 garlic clove
- ¼ cup olive oil
- ¼ head broccoli
- ¼ cup show peas
- ½ cup carrots
- ¼ cup green beans
- 1 tablespoon soy sauce
- ½ cup onion

DIRECTIONS

1. In a bowl combine garlic, olive oil, cornstarch and mix well
2. Add the rest of the ingredients and toss to coat
3. In a skillet cook vegetables mixture until tender
4. When ready transfer to a plate garnish with ginger and serve

SMOOTHIES

PROBIOTIC SMOOTHIE

Serves: *1*
Prep Time: *5* Minutes

Cook Time: *5* Minutes

Total Time: ***10*** Minutes

INGREDIENTS

- **1 pear**
- **¼ cup almond milk**
- **1 cup Greek yogurt**
- **1 tsp cinnamon**
- **1 cup ice**

DIRECTIONS

1. **In a blender place all ingredients and blend until smooth**
2. **Pour smoothie in a glass and serve**

ENERGY BOOSTING SMOOTHIE

Serves: *1*

Prep Time: *5* Minutes

Cook Time: *5* Minutes

Total Time: *10* Minutes

INGREDIENTS

- **1 banana**
- **1 pear**
- **1 avocado**
- **1 cup spinach**
- **1 cup ice**

DIRECTIONS

1. **In a blender place all ingredients and blend until smooth**
2. **Pour smoothie in a glass and serve**

BLUEBERRY SMOOTHIE

Serves: *1*
Prep Time: *5* Minutes
Cook Time: *5* Minutes
Total Time: *10* Minutes

INGREDIENTS

- **1 cup almond milk**
- **¼ cup Greek yogurt**
- **¼ tsp vanilla extract**
- **1 tsp honey**
- **1 cup kale**
- **¼ cup baby spinach**
- **1 cup blueberries**

DIRECTIONS

1. **In a blender place all ingredients and blend until smooth**
2. **Pour smoothie in a glass and serve**

RED CAPSICUM JUICE

Serves: *1*
Prep Time: *5* Minutes

Cook Time: *5* Minutes

Total Time: ***10*** Minutes

INGREDIENTS

- **1 cup red capsicum**
- **1 cup carrot**
- **1 cup apple**
- **1 cup ice**

DIRECTIONS

1. **In a blender place all ingredients and blend until smooth**
2. **Pour smoothie in a glass and serve**

GREEN SMOOTHIE

Serves: *1*

Prep Time: *5* Minutes

Cook Time: *5* Minutes

Total Time: *10* Minutes

INGREDIENTS

- **1 tablespoon tyrosine**
- **½ cup kale**
- **½ cup watercress**
- **¼ cup spinach**
- **¼ cup antioxidants**
- **1 cup ice**

DIRECTIONS

1. **In a blender place all ingredients and blend until smooth**
2. **Pour smoothie in a glass and serve**

RASPBERRY MOJITO FRAPPE

Serves: *1*
Prep Time: *5* Minutes

Cook Time: *5* Minutes

Total Time: *10* Minutes

INGREDIENTS

- **1 cup raspberries**
- **4-5 mint leaves**
- **1 tsp maple syrup**
- **1 cup ice**

DIRECTIONS

1. **In a blender place all ingredients and blend until smooth**
2. **Pour smoothie in a glass and serve**

MANGO SMOOTHIE

Serves: *1*

Prep Time: *5* Minutes

Cook Time: *5* Minutes

Total Time: ***10*** Minutes

INGREDIENTS

- **1 cup milk**
- **1 passionfruit**
- **1 banana**
- **1 mango**
- **1 tsp chia seeds**

DIRECTIONS

1. **Blend the ingredients together except the passion fruit**
2. **Serve topped with passionfruit seeds**

PINEAPPLE SMOOTHIE

Serves: *1*

Prep Time: *5* Minutes

Cook Time: *5* Minutes

Total Time: *10* Minutes

INGREDIENTS

- **1 cup apricot nectar**
- **1 banana**
- **½ mango**
- **Pineapple**

DIRECTIONS

1. **Mix everything together until smooth**
2. **Serve immediately**

BLUEBERRIES SMOOTHIE

Serves: *1*

Prep Time: *5* Minutes

Cook Time: *5* Minutes

Total Time: *10* Minutes

INGREDIENTS

- **1 banana**
- **Blueberries**
- **Milk**
- **1 mango**

DIRECTIONS

1. **Blend everything together until smooth**
2. **Serve immediately**

PEANUT BUTTER & BANANA SMOOTHIE

Serves: *1*
Prep Time: *5* Minutes

Cook Time: *5* Minutes

Total Time: *10* Minutes

INGREDIENTS

- 1 banana
- 1 cup coconut milk
- ¼ cup peanut butter
- 1 tablespoon honey
- 1 cup ice

DIRECTIONS

1. **In a blender place all ingredients and blend until smooth**
2. **Pour smoothie in a glass and serve**

GROOVY SMOOTHIE

Serves: *1*
Prep Time: *5* Minutes

Cook Time: *5* Minutes

Total Time: *10* Minutes

INGREDIENTS

- 1 banana
- 1 cup grapes
- ¼ cup Greek yogurt
- ¼ apple
- 1 cup baby spinach

DIRECTIONS

1. **In a blender place all ingredients and blend until smooth**
2. **Pour smoothie in a glass and serve**

THANK YOU FOR READING THIS BOOK!

CPSIA information can be obtained
at www.ICGtesting.com
Printed in the USA
BVHW030632260321
603505BV00001B/24

9 781664 05579